MASTERING YOUR THOUGHTS

Mind-Hacks No One's Talking About, Detachment Secrets and How to Kick Inner Emotions Into High Gear

STACY L. RAINIER

CONTENTS

Introduction	vii
1. IS YOUR LIFE A SELF-MADE MENTAL HELL?	1
Types of Negative Thoughts	1
Introduction to Obsessive Compulsive Disorder (OCD)	7
Anxiety	10
Depression	10
The Price of Negative Thoughts	12
2. AN INTRODUCTION TO NATURAL TECHNIQUES FOR ENDING NEGATIVE THINKING	15
Herbal Remedies	16
Diet	17
Mindfulness Meditation	18
Yoga	20
Acupuncture	21
EFT Tapping	21
3. SELF-ACTUALIZATION AND THE PATH TO FULFILLMENT	25
Preparation to Start Towards Self-Actualization	26
The Five Points of Self-Actualization	28
Characteristics of a Self-Actualized Person	30
17 Tips to Help With Self-Actualization	33
4. DETACHMENT: TAKE THE BY-PASS ROUTE AND ESCAPE THE BUSY FREEWAY OF YOUR MIND	39
Living in the Moment	40
You Ego: How It's Inhibiting Your Thoughts	41
Daily Tips to Free Your Busy Mind, Control Your Ego, and Detach When Necessary	47

5. DETACHMENT FROM WHAT NO LONGER SERVES YOU — 51
    Identifying Negative Influences in Your Life — 52
    Your Options to Approaching Negative Influences — 55

6. EMOTIONAL INTELLIGENCE AND HEALING YOUR INNER CHILD — 64
    Why Is Emotional Intelligence Valuable? — 66
    What Is Your Inner Child Saying? — 67
    Dealing with Triggers — 69

7. THE BEAUTY OF SELF-FORGIVENESS, SELF-COMPASSION, AND SELF-LOVE — 73
    Self-Forgiveness: Let the Healing Begin — 74
    Self-Love — 76
    Self-Compassion — 77

8. PUTTING YOURSELF FIRST IS NOT SELFISH — 80
    Learning to Prioritize You — 81
    Defining Your Core Values — 83

9. IT'S TIME TO REPROGRAM YOUR BRAIN — 86
    Techniques for Retraining — 88
    Self-Discipline — 94

10. AMAZING MEDITATION TECHNIQUES TO MASTER YOUR THOUGHTS — 95
    Technique 1: Concentration Meditation — 96
    Technique 2: Mindfulness Meditation — 98
    Technique 3: Walking Meditation — 99
    Technique 4: Chakra Meditation — 101

11. THE 10 STEP DAILY EMPOWERMENT RITUAL FOR MASTERY OF YOUR THOUGHTS — 104
    My 10 Step Secret Routine for Success: — 105

    Afterword — 107
    References — 111

© **Copyright 2021 - All rights reserved.**

The content contained within this book may not be reproduced, duplicated or transmitted without direct written permission from the author or the publisher.

Under no circumstances will any blame or legal responsibility be held against the publisher, or author, for any damages, reparation, or monetary loss due to the information contained within this book, either directly or indirectly.

Legal Notice:

This book is copyright protected. It is only for personal use. You cannot amend, distribute, sell, use, quote or paraphrase any part, or the content within this book, without the consent of the author or publisher.

Disclaimer Notice:

Please note the information contained within this document is for educational and entertainment purposes only. All effort has been executed to present accurate, up to date, reliable, complete information. No warranties of any kind are declared or implied. Readers acknowledge that the author is not engaged in the rendering of legal, financial, medical or professional advice. The content within this book has been derived from various sources. Please consult a licensed professional before attempting any techniques outlined in this book.

By reading this document, the reader agrees that under no circumstances is the author responsible for any losses, direct or indirect, that are incurred as a result of the use of the information contained within this document, including, but not limited to, errors, omissions, or inaccuracies.

INTRODUCTION

For many years I lived a life of self-doubt, anxiety, regret, guilt, and helplessness. I let negativity creep in and rule every aspect of my life. I learned to smile, laugh, and portray a positive exterior, but my mind worked full time to remind me that it was all a show. In many ways, I hated myself and lived a life so much less than I knew I was capable of. Does this sound familiar?

I have a very vivid memory of being on vacation. We saved for a year to be able to go. It was a dream of ours to rent a home on the beach in California. We wanted to take the family to Disneyland, eat at amazing restaurants, and lounge on the beach. We planned the vacation for months. We packed weeks before we left, that's how excited we were!

It was our third day of vacation, and it had been the best time we ever had. It could not have been more perfect. We were upgraded to first class on our flight, our house was even nicer than we expected, and the weather was beautiful. We were laying on the beach and I should have been enjoying everything and basking in the wonderful experience. Instead, my inner thoughts were that I looked overweight in the

INTRODUCTION

photos. I was anxious about being a victim of a random crime. I was worried constantly about our family's safety. And I couldn't stop stressing about the finances even though I knew we had planned for it. I seemed incapable of enjoying anything and it put me in a bad mood because I was so angry at myself. What was wrong with me?

That vacation was a pivotal moment for me. I was so tired of living in a state of negativity. At home I was able to convince myself that it was normal. I was functioning on an everyday basis; I had a great career and lots of friends. I had convinced myself that I was just a negative person and that it was totally normal. If I stayed positive on the outside, it wasn't a big deal. As long as my inner thoughts weren't pushed outward, I felt like I wasn't doing any harm. I was fine.

However, when I was in paradise and unable to enjoy it, I was not able to push down my doubts anymore. I was struggling with anxiety, depression, and negative self-talk. I realized more than ever that I wanted to change this, but I had no idea where to start.

MY STARTING POINT

When I decided to make a change for myself, I didn't realize the path I was starting down. I genuinely thought that my inner thoughts, as horrible and awful as they could be, weren't affecting my health and my life on a grand scale. I thought they were no big deal, and perhaps I didn't really need much change. I thought that if I could lower my stress levels a bit, and learn to be a bit more positive, I would be fine. I couldn't have been more wrong.

My research and journey made me aware of what my thoughts were doing to me both physically and emotionally. I had no idea that, by not taking them more seriously, I was damaging myself more and more each day. There were so many miraculous things that have changed as I have learned to master my thoughts.

Since my resolution to work on my inner self, I have seen changes within my life that I couldn't have anticipated:

1. My sleep has improved and I don't wake up tired as often as I used to.
2. I get sick much less.
3. I have lost weight.
4. I am more flexible with my schedule because I respond better to uncertainty.
5. My posture and demeanor have changed so much that I get comments on it regularly.
6. My energy levels are much higher.
7. I feel less "brain fog," and operate on a much higher level of productivity.
8. I'm more social
9. My relationships and connections with loved ones have deepened in ways I didn't know they could
10. I have a general sense of lightness. The best way I can explain it is the old standby of "a weight has been lifted off my shoulders," or, more accurately, my heart.

This list goes on and on about how much better I feel when it comes to my day to day.

My starting point when I wanted to feel better was simply by researching, "How can I make myself a more positive person?" I quickly moved onto other searches such as:

- How can I feel better about myself?
- Techniques for thinking more positively
- How can I make my inner emotions happier?

INTRODUCTION

- Ways to help with anxiety, depression, and OCD.

The answers that I received were a variety of medical opinions, spiritual offerings, and emotional healing techniques that have helped transform me into a new version of myself. I feel healed and cleansed. I am living the best way I know how, and I attribute it to all of the reasons I will share with you throughout the book.

My best advice when it comes to learning new paths in your journey to self-help is to be patient with yourself. You are an amazing individual! Taking the time to read this book tells me that you are ready for a change like I was. So be kind to yourself, and give yourself time to adapt to new ways of thinking.

Each time I tried a new technique or method of mastering my thoughts, I would give myself anywhere from two weeks up to two months to really focus on how it could help me retrain my brain. And I certainly wasn't done after two months, that was just a starting point to decide if a technique was going to be beneficial to me personally. Then the ongoing work starts to make this a lifelong process. So whatever it is that you need to help get you where you want to be, take it and don't look back.

I

IS YOUR LIFE A SELF-MADE MENTAL HELL?

My vacation story is only one small example of what my life was like. I would lay in bed at night unable to sleep because I would replay situations over and over in my head. I would fixate on things that had happened that day, that month, or even years prior. I would stress about conversations I had with people I barely knew. Even worse, I would think about things I saw in the news or on TV and be terrified that horrible things could happen to me and my family. Any situation that should have been positive, I would flip to think about all the negative things that could wreck it. When I reflect back on what my daily thoughts were, I wonder how I ever justified that as normal?

TYPES OF NEGATIVE THOUGHTS

Dr. David Burns discusses 10 types of negative thought in his book *Feeling Good: The New Mood Therapy* (2008). Also seen as "cognitive disorders," seeing these 10 types of negative thoughts was extremely eye opening for me. It immediately put me at ease that I wasn't alone in my way of thinking. I could put a name and an explanation to what I was doing, and also begin the process to start changing it.

I'll discuss the 10 types of thinking now as Dr. Burns describes them:

1. **All or Nothing**: This style or thinking (also referred to as "Black and White thinking") is the idea that you either do something exactly the way you expect it to happen and at full force, or you just give up. I approached everything with this mentality. I felt that if I couldn't devote large amounts of time to something, I wouldn't even bother. And then I would get upset or stressed that I hadn't done anything! It's very unrealistic and sets you up for inevitable failure. An example of this style of thinking would be if you started a new workout plan. You made a big goal of going from no workouts, to five workouts/week. If you even miss one, you just quit because either you commit fully or it's not worth it in your mind.
2. **Overgeneralization**: This style of thinking happens when one event or thought causes a person to think that's the way it always is. They create a huge generalization from one instance. An example would be if you have a really uneventful month. Work is normal, nothing too exciting happening there. You see friends a few times. You aren't too social or spending too much time alone. Your health is great. No sickness to report. Nothing is out of the ordinary except at the end of the month you receive a speeding ticket in the mail. It's going to cost you a lot of money. Your thoughts immediately start to spiral. "Of course

this would happen to me, I always have the worst luck," or "What a terrible month this has been." Even though nothing bad happened all month, you overgeneralize because of one thing. Think about these statements you may have thought about:

- "Nothing good ever happens to me."
- "I never win at anything."
- "Some people have all the luck."

1. **Mental Filter**: A mental filter is when you tend to pick out and focus on the small negative details in what should be a good situation, so the entire situation is perceived as negative. An example would be if you had a great night out for dinner. The conversation was great, food was good, and the service was fantastic. As you get up to leave the restaurant, you slip and fall. No one else in your group even gives it a second thought after they realize you are okay. After you get home, the only thing you focus on is how silly you looked, and how embarrassed you feel, and you forget about the rest of the night.
2. **Disqualifying the Positive**: This type of thinking basically renders you incapable of taking compliments or positive feedback. If someone were to say to you "Wow you did a great job on that project," your response would be, "I think I got lucky." You see things that you do positively as a one time thing, or compliments as something that aren't true.
3. **Jumping to Conclusions**: This type of thinking is when we assume things about what other people are thinking, or situations that have happened, or

even predict things before they have occurred. An example would be if your friend cancels plans with you at the last minute without much explanation. You assume that it must be because they are mad at you and you spend days trying to figure out what went wrong, and create a whole story in your head. Then after a few days up, they call you up to apologize for canceling but they had to go help a family member in another city with an emergency situation. You spent days of energy fretting about something that didn't even happen.

4. **Magnification and Minimization**: This type of cognitive disorder refers to our abilities to magnify situations and minimize others depending on which one will have a more negative outcome. With this type of thinking, you can take a situation and minimize something positive you did while also magnifying one small negative detail to center that into your take-away thoughts. Let's say that you have a performance review at work. Your superior goes over all the wonderful things that you are accomplishing in your position, and references one small negative that they wish you would take more initiative to be a leader within your coworkers. In your head, you would completely minimize the twenty positive things they said, and magnify this one piece of constructive feedback to be a negative that you aren't good at your job and have no future there.

5. **Emotional Reasoning**: This is the idea that your emotions can dictate reality. You allow your emotions to cloud your ability to think rationally. An example would be if you start to get a little down about your relationship with your

significant other. Rather than being reasonable, which might sound like "We haven't been getting along lately. We've both been so busy at work, we should try and make some time for each other." You might have more emotional thoughts like "We haven't been getting along for forever, we've drifted apart. What if they don't love me anymore?" You know in your mind that it's not the case, but you just let your emotions take over.

6. **Should Statements**: You give yourself orders and goals by creating "should" and "shouldn't" statements. "I should workout more." "I should be a better friend." "I shouldn't stress so much." They are statements that are usually vague, full of pressure, and set unrealistic expectations for yourself. Should statements usually set you up for failure.

7. **Labeling and Mislabeling**: This behavior is when you give labels to yourself, other people, or perhaps even situations. It makes it very difficult for you to see past the labels, and most likely the label was an unfair assessment in the first place. An example would be if you were taking a cooking class. On the first day, you burned something in the oven, so you label yourself a bad cook. You made one small mistake, and instead of recognizing that you are a good cook that did something wrong, you add a label to all of your abilities. The same goes for other people. Maybe, because the teacher of that cooking class made a mistake and told you the wrong temperature on the oven, so you label them as a bad teacher. It's an unfair label, and then you close yourself off to fully

learning from them because you have an unfair assessment of their abilities.
8. **Personalization**: This is when you make yourself responsible for external events. You will blame yourself for things that aren't your cause. An example would be if your friend invited you to grab a drink on a patio. The weather turns really badly, so you both have to cancel. Your friend seems disappointed and you blame yourself and feel really bad even though the weather is out of your control. You put the blame and guilt on yourself.

After you see these types of thoughts explained in a simple way, are there any that particularly resonate with you? Do all of them resonate with you? There's no wrong answer here. It's just being aware of those particular negative practices that you may be guilty of.

Being able to see an explanation of all these types of negative thoughts gave me instant clarity and relief. I suddenly didn't feel hopeless in a cloud of negative thoughts. I could now separate out certain recurring thoughts and recognize what they were. All of a sudden, my inner dialogue had context. If I had a thought like "This is going to be an awful week," I could immediately label it as the type of negative thought "jumping to conclusions" and try to rethink my approach heading into the week. All of a sudden it wasn't just me being a negative person anymore, it was me being able to identify my thoughts and actively label them and correct them.

Becoming more aware of what I had been doing to myself, I realized that I truly had turned my inner thoughts into a negative and emotionally draining hell. It impacted so much more of my life than I was aware of, and I was shocked that I let it go on for so long. Why on earth was I doing that to myself, and continuing to do it to myself? What was it specifically that was driving this type of behavior within me? My ongoing journey of self-improvement led me to learn about Obsessive Compulsive Disorder (OCD).

INTRODUCTION TO OBSESSIVE COMPULSIVE DISORDER (OCD)

I think everyone has heard the term OCD before. I had a misguided understanding of what it meant, and certainly didn't think it applied to me. I had only seen it referencing individuals who wanted things neat, tidy, or who obsessed over repetitive behaviors like locking doors 10 times. OCD is much more than that, and my thought patterns were very much a behavior that fell into this diagnosis.

The American Psychiatric Association defines OCD as "a disorder in which people have recurring, unwanted thoughts, ideas or sensations (obsessions) that make them feel driven to do something repetitively (compulsions)" ("What Is Obsessive-Compulsive Disorder?" 2009).

What I realized is that I associated OCD with the compulsive part, and didn't realize that my negative thoughts were a condition of the obsessive component that can affect people. I was consumed by the same types of thoughts, and patterns of responding to things, and didn't know how to break it.

People without OCD can naturally have bothersome thoughts, but the difference of how negative thinking becomes a disorder is when those thoughts disrupt your everyday life. If the thoughts prevent you from living the way you should, then you have a problem.

This was my scenario. When I was younger, I labeled myself a worrier. I would lay awake at night and worry about things that may or may not happen. If I had something due at school I couldn't relax until it was handed in. I worried about getting into trouble, getting sick and missing things. I even worried about getting into trouble because of a misunderstanding and being blamed for something I didn't do. I remember a teacher calling me a "worry wart," as if that's not the most unattractive name ever. I accepted it as who I was, and that it wasn't something I needed to change. I was a worrier, no big deal.

As I got older, my patterns never changed. The only difference now was that I had bigger things to worry about: bills, my job, relationships, and more. I would get very overwhelmed at times, and often retreat from social situations on weekends to give myself a chance to recover from the week's interactions and thoughts. Then I would worry about not seeing people. Would they be mad at me? Would they continue to keep inviting me out if I always declined? I couldn't seem to find a balance anymore between being a worrier and still being happy. The worrying took on a life of its own, and most of it became negative which led to me feeling negative about myself. Even reading back about it exhausts me when I remember how drained I felt all the time.

As I had a family, things took on a completely new level. I had to learn to function because being a parent requires a lot of different skills. I was able to put the needs of my little one's before my own when it came to retreating from situations. Being so busy at all times helped because I didn't have as much downtime for my thoughts to take over. However, when I did have time to just think, it got ugly. My worrying turned into full blown anxiety and it prevented me from sleeping. This would cause me to be less attentive during the day. Then I would feel anxiety and mild depression that I wasn't being a great parent, and that I wasn't giving a top performance at work. I had plenty of things to overanalyze because I never felt like I was doing anything right. It was an endless cycle.

I learned to put on a face, and push the thoughts down. Other areas started to fall apart instead. You know that image where you have a leak somewhere, so you cover it with a finger. It stops for a moment, but the water finds its way out somewhere else. So you cover that water with another finger, and so on. Eventually you run out of fingers to stop the water and it gets out anyway. I managed to push my negative thoughts down, or aside, and cover them up. It worked for a while, but eventually it needed an outlet and, as a result, my negative energy funneled out in the form of Binge eating disorder and I gained a lot of weight.

It took me gaining a lot of weight for my doctor to take notice that something wasn't operating right. My physical condition was now really suffering as a result of my mental struggles. My eating was a side effect of my deeper condition of OCD. The weight gain and my epiphany on our family vacation were the pushes that I needed to start exploring options to heal myself.

Although we have touched on depression, anxiety, OCD, and other emotional disorders, there is so much more to discuss in arming yourself to fight the war against them. For most of us, it will be an ongoing battle that we will fight for the rest of our lives. The exciting news is that it will get easier.

In the beginning, if you look at your disorder when it's at its most powerful moment, it is a formidable opponent. But over time as you get stronger, your opponent will get weaker and smaller. As you grow, your disorder will lose its power with each tool and skill you learn to fight them. What once was an unfair fight with you on the losing side, turns the table to give you the advantage.

Even though we may always be a little prone to suffering

from these ailments throughout our lives, by taking the time to learn how to treat them you are giving yourself a lifelong gift to win.

ANXIETY

Anxiety is a heightened state of stress. Our body responds to stress, fear, discomfort, uncertainty, and other emotionally charged feelings with an increased worry response. It's perfectly healthy and normal to feel anxious before events or certain situations; a job interview, or running into an ex would be good examples. It's when the level of that worry, and the frequency becomes overwhelming that it has negative consequences.

Our body's natural response to uncertainty and fear is to protect itself with hormonal and sensory reactions. You have probably heard of the "fight or flight" response that is inherent within us. When your body is pushed into this state too often and for too long, it becomes both mentally and physically unhealthy. Your body is not meant to feel that type of intensity for long durations; it needs to relax and calm itself to heal from those experiences.

There are many types of anxiety disorders that range from phobias, social anxiety disorders, to post traumatic stress disorder (PTSD). OCD falls under the category of an anxiety disorder as well, so you can see how my thoughts and cognitive behaviors are all connected.

DEPRESSION

Words that are associated with depression are sadness, unmotivated, antisocial, and down. Although these are all accurate, it doesn't fully depict the volume to which they apply. Depression is an all encompassing state of these feelings.

Your emotions have spiraled so low that your physical state suffers as well. It is not just being sad and crying. Depression can be when you cry multiple times a day and are often unsure why. Your body aches with overwhelming feelings of despair. It can present itself in a variety of ways, but the one common theme is that it is debilitating to be able to enjoy your life and everything in it.

There are a lot of causes for depression, such as:

Family: Depression can be genetic and is often something seen shared between family members. It's not to say that you are guaranteed to suffer from it if a parent does, but being aware of their history can help you identify if it affects you.

Traumatic event: A tragic event such as a sudden loss can trigger depression. Coping with such events is extremely difficult and your mind can shut down without the proper tools to do so.

Childhood or ongoing trauma: Events from our childhood or ongoing exposure to a really negative source can cause depression as it manifests in us. Not coping with the source leaves us open to negative self-talk and lower self-esteem.

Negative thoughts and OCD: when your thoughts get to the level that we talked about in earlier chapters, your mindset can spiral into a place of depression in addition to your OCD and anxiety. The overwhelming thoughts that occupy every waking moment can become a lot to handle and cause grief to be added to your mental state.

There are many options for treatment of depression, and doing your research to decide what is best for you is very important. There is no one right answer in terms of a correct path to treatment of depression. My personal experience has been with anxiety and OCD, which I have always sought the natural path. My experience with depression is not thorough. It has augmented my other disorders, but I cannot say that I have been completely consumed with it the way others suffer.

That being said, I am familiar with using natural methods to relieve emotional disorders and lessen the power of their grip. In the next chapter and later on in the book we will go over methods and techniques in detail to help free your mind of its cognitive disorders and reprogram your mindset to help you grow and develop into a healthier version of yourself.

THE PRICE OF NEGATIVE THOUGHTS

I think we underestimate the power of our thoughts both positive and negative. It affects every aspect of our lives. Our personal relationships, creativity, work, physical wellbeing, and emotional health. I've lived it and I've seen it through other people. When your systems are working irregularly or your mind is blocked with negativity, it affects you in ways you might not realize.

Relationships: Negative thoughts will spill into your relationship. Even if it's not negative thoughts directed at your partner, your ongoing negativity will wear on them. You might not even be aware of it. But if the majority of your interactions are negative, like complaining constantly, having a poor outlook on things, or upset about something that happened, then your partner will become overwhelmed and exhausted. They may not be able to handle it long-term and will withdraw to save themselves.

Creativity: Your creative light comes from within. When your meridians are all in alignment, and your energy can flow freely throughout your body without the blockages of negative thoughts, anxiety, depression, or OCD, your creativity will be in full force. The opposite will happen when you allow your thoughts to consume you. Your creative light will dim, and it can be hard to find it when you need it.

Work: Your work life can suffer due to negativity and lack of control of your thoughts. It can be hard for your coworkers to be around you and create a positive work environment. People may start to avoid you and pass you over for promotions or certain opportunities. Even if you are great at masking your negativity and staying professional, it can be hard to stay motivated when your mind is consumed.

Physical: We've discussed this a little already, but your physical body can suffer immensely due to an imbalance in your mental state. Your sleep is affected which in turn can open you up to illness. When you are tired, it can be even harder to change your thought patterns and start to heal. It's a very difficult cycle. When you are negative and suffering physically, it will start to affect your overall physical wellbeing. You may start to notice pains due to poor posture, lack of desire for physical intimacy, and ongoing sickness with a weaker immune system.

Emotional: This may be the most obvious repercussion of negative thought patterns, anxiety, depression, and OCD. With your thoughts feeling out of control, your emotions can feel like they aren't your own. I remember there being times when I felt angry or sad and I felt helpless to change it. I didn't want to feel that way, and I recognized that I had no reason to feel that way, but I was powerless to adjust it. It was horrible. My vacation story in the beginning is an example of this. I knew I should've felt blissful and happy, but was incapable of it.

If you are feeling overwhelmed at this moment, I apologize. Going through this type of information can be daunting and slightly disheartening. You can feel like it's too much to conquer when you are up against a mountain. I sure did.

But here is the GREAT news: You have the power to change it!

Repeat that to yourself again. You have the power to change your thoughts. You don't have to accept that you are "just a negative person" or "a worry wart." Your mind is the most powerful tool known to mankind. I believe that you can beat this, because I did it. I shattered my mental imprisonment of negative thoughts, destructive self-talk, OCD tendencies, and general hopelessness.

I recognized the negativity within myself as the enemy, and decided to arm myself with the weapons I needed to go to war with it, and blast it down to a presence I was comfortable with. We are about to discuss a variety of natural treatment methods to get you started on your path. As you begin your journey, try them all. Give them all a few weeks of practice because change doesn't come overnight, and you need a bit of time to decide if it's going to be effective for you. You are a powerful person, and you can master your thoughts with these tools and win the war. Throughout this book, you are going to learn about yourself, your abilities, and the potential of what you can become.

2
AN INTRODUCTION TO NATURAL TECHNIQUES FOR ENDING NEGATIVE THINKING

Treating any kind of mental illness naturally is not a path for everyone, but it was the right path for me. It takes a lot of commitment and hard work. It's a long process that can be frustrating at times, so you have to promise yourself that you will see it through to the point where you see change and progress.

We will save detailed practices and techniques till the end of the book. However, getting an introduction to these techniques provides you with a starting point, and the beginning of a plan to soak in all of the knowledge you will read throughout the book. Seeing how these natural techniques play into your development will excite and motivate you to begin your journey.

HERBAL REMEDIES

There are a variety of herbal remedies that patients have found great success in treating OCD. As with any types of changes to supplements or diet, it's always best to talk with your doctor to make sure you have a green light to proceed with taking a new remedy.

Owen Kelly PhD sites the following options as potential herbal options to help with your OCD (2020):

- St. John's Wort: An herbal supplement used to help with serotonin levels. Quite often used to treat anxiety, depression, and OCD which are all linked to irregular serotonin levels.
- Milk Thistle: This has been used in other countries for many years in the treatment of depression.
- N-Acetylcysteine: This helps moderate glutamine production in the brain. It contributes to the

overall health of your brain and can decrease the symptoms of OCD.

DIET

When it comes to your health, your diet can create issues that you didn't even realize were food based. Remember how I said my eating spiraled as a result of me ignoring my mental health? The situation got even worse because the foods that I was eating can actually exacerbate anxiety, depression, and OCD. I felt horrible, out of control, and unable to fix things. The impact of what you eat is amazing. We forget how eating healthy and nourishing our bodies moves way past physical benefits. Our brain is just as much a part of our physical bodies as our bones and muscles, and feeding it with fresh wonderful food is essential to feel good mentally as well.

Eating a well-balanced diet of healthy proteins, fruits, vegetables, low fat dairy, and whole grains will give your body and, more importantly, your brain everything it needs to operate at optimal performance.

Staying away from processed foods, sugars, high saturated fats, and alcohol will prevent your systems from becoming unbalanced and dysfunctional.

I like to think of myself as a beautiful plant. As a plant, you know the nutrients you need to stay healthy are sun and lots of clean, fresh water. If you decide to sit in the dark, and drink soda all day, as a plant you would wither away. As a person, when you don't feed your body with all the nutrients it needs, you are the equivalent of that plant. You can't be strong physically and mentally to fight off invading physical and mental ailments.

MINDFULNESS MEDITATION

Mindfulness meditation is the method of using various breathing techniques and guided imagery to be acutely aware of your feelings in the moment. It brings awareness to your deepest thoughts and emotions without judgement or analysis. It helps to lower your stress levels and relax ("Mindfulness Exercises," 2020).

There are many benefits to mindfulness meditation. What seems like a simple exercise, and may feel like you're doing nothing is wildly beneficial to your mind and body. The evidence behind meditation suggests that it lowers stress, anxiety, pain, depression, and insomnia. It has the benefits of better mental clarity, better sleep, and decreasing burnout ("Mindfulness Exercises," 2020).

There are a variety of resources to help you practice mindful meditation. There are apps on your phone, online programs, and local courses. It doesn't have to be difficult or be on a strict schedule. You just need to take time and have a quiet place to get into touch with your inner self-and emotions. As with all new skills, practice will make you better and better over time.

In the beginning, your mind will naturally wander. The practice seems easy, but letting go of your everyday thoughts can be very difficult and doesn't happen automatically. Be kind to yourself and don't get frustrated. I have dabbled in guided meditation, but I find the following technique to be the most effective for me:

1. First I pour myself a tall glass of cold water. I'll explain what I use that for later.
2. I make myself a quiet and comfortable spot to lay down. I prefer to lay down while I meditate

because it calms me and allows me to fully relax. Usually I just lay on my bed with a cool fan on.
3. I set an alarm for 30 min in case I fall asleep to make sure I don't lose track of time. It happens sometimes. I might not get all the benefits of meditation every time when I fall asleep but it usually makes me feel amazing when I do. And I want to respect what my body needs, so I just let it happen.
4. Depending on how the weather is outside, I either put a hot or cold cloth on my head. I quite often put a few drops of essential oils on the cloth to create an extra level of sensory calmness.
5. I focus my thoughts on my breath. I breathe in to the count of five and breathe out for the count of five. I focus on relaxing everything in my body. I try to sink into the bed and feel the tension go out of my hands and feet. I relax my muscles, even the facial muscles, and concentrate on breathing in and out for as long as I can.
6. If I find my mind drifting or concentrating on something other than breathing, I take a sip of water to refocus and start my relaxation and breathing all over again.
7. If I need to work through something, mediation is a time that I can calmly think things through. If I have a problem that I am struggling with, I focus my thoughts around my breathing. Let's say I am having an argument with my spouse and I find my thoughts to be spiraling in a negative direction. I can use mindful meditation to change my mindset. I will breathe in and think of something positive. I imagine that I am breathing in positive energy and

thoughts about my partner. Then when I exhale I imagine myself pushing out the negative thoughts and energy. The longer I breathe positive images and thoughts in, the less upset I feel and can approach the situation more calmly and in a better head space. I find it works with all types of problems.

Mindfulness meditation is a powerful tool when it comes to mastering your thoughts, emotions and cognitive disorders. Being able to practice on a daily basis strengthens your ability to work through your negative thoughts and balance them. Meditating is comparable to exercising your muscles. The more you do it, the stronger your brain becomes.

YOGA

Many people look at yoga as a fitness option for physical health. It absolutely has physical benefits, but it is also meant to be a practice to align your physical, emotional, and mental self-through movement and breathing. Similar to meditation, it increases your ability to cope with your emotions and gain control of your thoughts. For many people, having the connection to the body and movement creates a stronger connection than mediation alone, but it's your journey and you need to decide what works for you.

I personally have always had more success with meditation alone because I find myself more likely to practice it everyday, thus getting more benefits than if I only did it a few times a week. Try each method and find what speaks to you and your needs. Try to be aware of your mental state as you come out of yoga or meditation sessions and try to see which one makes you feel like your best self.

ACUPUNCTURE

Acupuncture works amazingly for therapy as well. This ancient Chinese practice uses needles to align to different systems of the body. The acupuncturist is able to identify imbalances to restore the body back to full function. Acupuncture looks to find the root of the problem. OCD is a condition of something else that is working incorrectly, and by strengthening that system, it decreases the symptoms that accompany cognitive disorders and other emotion based issues (Molinoff, n.d.).

EFT TAPPING

Emotional Freedom Technique (EFT), is quite often also referred to as "tapping." It is the practice of physically tapping along your meridians or acupressure points to restore balance to one's emotional, physical, and mental alignment. The exciting thing about EFT is that it is easy to perform and has unparalleled reported results from practitioners. This is what drew me in.

When it came to my own treatment path, I knew three things about myself.

1. My body doesn't respond well to medication. If there are side effects associated with a medication, I seem to acquire them. I appreciate medication for having benefits of modern science, but I really prefer to use it as a last resort.
2. If a treatment requires me to go to appointments, I will eventually stop going. Time constraints and commitment are difficult for me, so to set myself up for success, I prefer to do something at home. For this reason, acupuncture did not seem like the

right fit for me. I have gone in the past for other reasons and will continue to use acupuncture in the future for other things, but for regular treatment of my OCD it didn't seem like the right fit.
3. If it's something I can do in smaller blocks of time, I will have a higher success rate. For this reason, I knew yoga couldn't be my main source of treatment. I knew once I did the research that my OCD, negative thought cycles, and emotional disorders would be best treated through mindfulness meditation and EFT.

You can do EFT anywhere. If you are stuck in traffic, waiting in line, at your desk, laying in bed, or watching TV. That's one of the main reasons why it has been extremely effective for me. I found it to be very calming as soon as I started it. It was almost like it helped redirect my anxious and negative feelings into the gentle tapping I was doing to the various tapping points. I can't stress enough how much it has helped me work through my OCD and continues to help guide me on an everyday basis when I need to think through something.

There are a variety of resources that can help teach you to "tap." Below is an overview list of the tapping points and what areas they represent and can help you with (Lyons, n.d.):

Tapping Location
Meridian
What it Releases
Treatment Benefit
Top of Head
100 Meeting Point Meridian
Your Inner Critic and lack of focus
Focus, clarity, insight, emotional connection

Eyebrow
Bladder Meridian
Frustration, pain, hurt, sadness, impatience, rejection, trauma
Emotional peace and centered healing
Side of Eye
Gall Bladder Meridian
Anger, resentment, rage, resistance to change
Understanding, calmness, and empathy
Under Eye
Stomach Meridian
Worry, emptiness, fear, anxiousness, and nervousness
Safety and calmness
Under Nose
Governing Meridian
Shame, fear, guilt, embarrassment, helplessness
Self-empowerment, self-acceptance, strength
Center of Chin
Central Meridian
Confusion, indecisiveness, frustration, anxious, lack of clarity
Focus, certainty, support, and calm
Collarbone
Kidney Meridian
Stress, worry, feeling stuck, unmotivated
motivation and confidence.
Under Arm
Spleen Meridian
Obsessing, insecurity, unhappy, and worry
Contentment, calm, focus, and security

THERE ARE MANY PROGRAMS, TECHNIQUES, AND METHODS to get the most out of tapping, but in the beginning I made mine very simple for myself. I would determine something that I wanted to focus on. For example, let's say I was feeling particularly anxious one day. I find that very windy days make me anxious. I would find the tapping point that coincides with those feelings and tap repeatedly while focusing on a positive thought in regards to what bothers me. In this situation I would gently tap the center of my chin and say to myself: "Wind is beautiful, wind is powerful, wind is nature's breath, I am safe in my home."

We will cover a longer sequence and a proven tapping method in Chapter 9.

3

SELF-ACTUALIZATION AND THE PATH TO FULFILLMENT

Self-actualization is the realization of one's true potential. Paying close attention to the fact that it is called self-actualization, there is no gauge or measurement to know when you are there. It's a very personal process, and no two people are alike. There are a lot of ways to describe self-actualization, but the one that resonated with me the most was this:

"Self-actualization can generally be thought of as the full realization of one's creative, intellectual, and social potential through internal drive (versus for external rewards like money, status, or power)." (Selva, 2019, para. 8)

How amazing does that sound? Having the ability to reach your full potential on all levels? I remember always feeling held back. I knew I could do more and be more, but couldn't seem to get the traction or keep the motivation to get there. I felt like years were passing by, and I was trapped. I had so many overgeneralized thoughts all the time. "I'll never get myself organized," or I would put things off, saying "someday I will get in shape and have more time to myself." I never actually believed that self-actualization was a possibility for me anytime soon. Combine that underlying thinking with my mental illnesses, and I was really working up against a few things. I look back on myself in that state, and I completely understand why I felt so hopeless.

PREPARATION TO START TOWARDS SELF-ACTUALIZATION

Now take that comparison of where I was and where I journeyed to and imagine how I felt when I looked around and realized that I had reached a place that I would consider self-actualization? I now feel free, accomplished, and more proud of myself than I ever have before.

On a day to day basis I am so much happier. I don't shy away from social situations, I feel more motivated to make healthier decisions, and my creative light can't be stopped.

We talked about different methods to help with cognitive disorders and negative thought patterns in Chapter 2. Working through that first is essential to get you into a head space where you are ready to progress forward into a state of self-actualization. That is a whole new level of self-reflection and happiness. Be gentle with your mental state and give yourself plenty of time to feel healthy and happy. Don't put any pressure on yourself to get to a "perfect" place. That's not what self-actualization is.

The concept of self-actualization gained its popularity through the psychologist Abraham Maslow and his theory titled Maslow's Hierarchy of Needs. His theory is that you need to take care of certain needs before you can move onto the next level of needs. If you don't satisfy all the needs of one level before you move to the next, you won't have the basic building blocks to become successful at the next point (Selva, 2019):

- At the lowest level is your physiological needs. These are the basic needs you require to survive. This would include your food, shelter, water, and rest. Only when you satisfy these needs can you move up to the next level successfully.
- The next level is safety and security.
- The third level is your belongingness and needs for love. This is having your social and physiological relationship needs met through family, romantic relationships and friendships.
- The fourth level is esteem needs. This is where you feel your sense of accomplishment and self-worth.
- The fifth and final level is our topic of conversation: self-actualization.

The theory has been popular for so long because it lends itself to understanding why sometimes we get stuck and can't move forward in our personal growth. If, for example, you lost your job and were worried about having a place to live, your focus wouldn't be able to move past that onto higher levels until you solved that problem. Once you had your shelter taken care of and you felt safe and secure, you could refocus on your psychological needs of level three and then four.

You can also see clearly now how if you are stuck on our topics in Chapter 1 and unable to move past level four, you may not have much success on our focus of level five. You don't have to be perfect at any time, but you need to feel secure enough on each level to have the head space, energy, and tools to attack the next level. When you feel strong enough and confident enough, you can begin the exciting journey of self-actualization.

THE FIVE POINTS OF SELF-ACTUALIZATION

It is commonly thought that there are five sections as a part of self-actualization. Let's get into them now.

1. Self-Awareness: This is a natural gift that not a lot of people have. It comes from being able to recognize your emotions, why you are feeling things, reasons for your behaviors, your personal traits (both good and bad), your desires, and your motivations. Becoming self-aware can sometimes come through therapy or asking for help from trusted family and friends. Sometimes it's hard for us to see certain things about ourselves, and hearing them from outside sources can help us get perspective.
2. Emotional Exploration: Trying to process your emotions, or even recognize what your emotions are, can be very difficult. I know at times I feel very irritable and I can't figure out why. There's that old saying that "you woke up on the wrong side of the bed." Sometimes you can be angry, or frustrated, or sad and you have no idea where it came from. Try to explore the emotions by mapping them out. I like to journal them to see if over time there are patterns. I like to answer the following questions everyday to get in touch with emotions that I can't quite communicate to myself.
3. How did I feel when I woke up?
4. How did I feel when I went to bed last night?
5. How did I sleep?
6. On a scale of 1-10, how high do I rank the intensity of the emotion?

7. Throughout the day, how long did it last, and what even changed my feelings?
8. What did the weather look like?

Interestingly enough, I added that last question after a month of journaling. I was reading about other people's journaling experiences and tips, and I found one story of a gentleman who noticed his moods coincided very closely to the weather. I found that very fascinating and decided to do the same. I found that certain patterns did arise with weather changes. Obviously we can't change the weather, but by knowing that my body is sensitive to weather changes, I can coach myself through it much better. Remember my anxiousness to the wind and my EFT approach. I can do similar methods to prepare myself with other weather changes as well.

1. Emotional Awareness: The findings that I discovered through emotional exploration is what brought me to emotional awareness. Being able to link my feelings to a cause, or understand what stimulus was able to move me into a different head space was not only eye opening but incredibly freeing. I felt more in control of my emotions than I ever had before. How exciting to not have to just throw my hands up and surrender to a bad mood, or chronic sadness, or fear, or anxiety. I was now learning tools to modify my emotions. However, the only reason these tools became effective was because I was aware of the emotions in the first place.
2. Highlighting Strengths: Make a list right now of all the things you think that you excel at. Don't be shy! No one is going to see this but you. So don't

be humble. Everything you've even been proud of, write it down. After you've written your own list, ask two or three friends what their suggestions are. I would be willing to bet that they see strength in you that you have no idea about. Hearing someone say something powerful about you can bring you a level of confidence and pride that you might not feel on your own. Not that you need outside validation, but having that perspective from someone who loves you is very touching.

3. Highlighting Weaknesses: This one isn't quite as fun, but very necessary. To really get to the point of full self-actualization, you need to be aware of your weaknesses. You have to accept everything about yourself. Flaws are a part of you, and you can learn to love them, or decide you want to work on them. Either way, you are beautiful, wonderful, and incredible.

We will move onto some tips on how to achieve these five areas of self-actualization momentarily, but first I want to go over what a self-actualized person looks like.

CHARACTERISTICS OF A SELF-ACTUALIZED PERSON

Everyone is going to have a different version of themselves as a self-actualized person. My best self-is not the same as everyone else's. But on a very general level, a self-actualized individual has some or many of the following characteristics (Raypole, 2020):

1. Independence: They live their lives for themselves, their own values, and their own approval. They don't look to outside sources for validation, and are confident spending time on their own.
2. A sense of happiness and humor: They find humor in most situations and don't take things too seriously. They have the ability to laugh at themselves.
3. Kindness and compassion: By being so comfortable and happy with themselves, they have the emotional availability to be patient, kind and compassionate with other people.
4. Grounded: They are realistic about most aspects of their life, and set realistic goals. They have a good grasp of their own self-awareness and different situations.
5. Creative and spontaneous: Self-actualized individuals have the ability to approach new situations with creativity and spontaneity. As well, with their meridians open and nothing blocking their creative channels, any artistic passions they have flow out of them.
6. Feel connected: They feel at peace with themselves and connected to a greater spiritual force or the universe depending on their beliefs.
7. See the world beyond themselves: They see the world as something beyond their existence and quite often contribute a lot of their time to helping

other people and different causes. They don't just focus on their own life and their own problems.
8. Compassionate: They have a longing to help other people and want to see the best for other people.
9. Enjoy the present: They have the ability to enjoy their current life and aren't always waiting for the next phase or for things to get better in some way. They can appreciate the small moments and slow down to savor little things.

Recognizing the point when you are "self-actualized" will be your own decision and feeling. When you look through the list above, you may have some of these characteristics already, but still not feel anywhere near a point where you are satisfied with who you are.

Being self-actualized for me boiled down to a few small things. And trust me when I say that I'm only partially there and it will be an ongoing journey for the rest of my life. It will be for all of us. For me, it comes down to the ability to be happy, and feel good about how I am living my life. I want to keep working towards a brighter, more fulfilled, optimistic, calm, and healthier version of my current state. I have come really far in my journey to get to a place that I would consider neutral. By working through EFT, and mindful meditation, I am not fully consumed by my OCD negative thoughts and anxiety. Now I am constantly developing myself to this dream of being a fully self-actualized person and working to stay that way.

Through my research, I've come across a lot of tips, and some of my own on how to work towards this goal.

17 TIPS TO HELP WITH SELF-ACTUALIZATION

1. Buy a journal: I mentioned that I used a journal before for documenting my mood to help analyze my feelings and how they affected me. I also use a journal to write down a lot of what I am thinking. Each day I try to write down one thing that was great about my day, one thing I struggled with, and something beautiful that I observed that had nothing to do with me.
2. Make a list of your favorite things, small joys, and keep adding to it: I keep this at the back of my journal. I started by writing down all the little things that I can think of that bring me small joys. And then, as I experience them, I add to the list. Things like pulling warm laundry on when you are chilly, sitting and watching your child play sports, snuggling up with tea and watching the snow. All of the different things that bring you moments of pure happiness.
3. Be patient: You aren't going to reinvent yourself overnight, so if you are struggling to find your happiness, emotional awareness, strengths, and weaknesses, don't get mad at yourself. You are fully capable of this, and don't ever stop to think otherwise.

4. Try new things: Pushing your boundaries can sometimes pull down walls or open up new emotional exploration. An example would be if you don't see yourself as a spontaneous person, and you give in to a spontaneous act and have an amazing time. Maybe you need to rethink your perception of yourself. Maybe you are a spontaneous individual!
5. Seek counseling or therapy: counselors, psychologists, and psychiatrists are all professionals trained in helping people with their self-awareness and emotional disorders. Sometimes having someone give you new terminology, or help in identifying what you are feeling, and what you are wanting to feel can be life changing. It's not for everyone, or in everyone's budget, but if you are willing and able to try it, what do you have to lose? There are also usually free services offered through local organizations and universities as well.
6. Love who you are: You have to learn to love who you are and how you act. It's so much easier said than done, but learning to care less about what people think is a big part of the self-actualization process. This is where I found my journaling to come in handy again. If I came home and was fretting about an interaction I had with someone, or upset about a situation that I was worried about what the other person was thinking, I would write it down. Similar to the idea that you've probably heard about writing out an email to someone if you are upset and then waiting a few days to send it, I would write out what I thought the interaction looked like and then I would wait a few days and reread it. It freed my mind to not think about it

anymore because I knew that I would look at the writing later. It's amazing when you put a bit of space between you and what you think happened, how differently you will feel when you reread it. A few days later when I had time to distance myself, I would quite often giggle at my own writing and how silly I was being.
7. Volunteer and put yourself in new situations: Volunteering and meeting new people can sometimes make you realize how appreciative you should be of where you are. When you are exposed to situations where someone else's focus is on a different level of needs such as food and shelter, it puts into perspective how wonderful your life is. In addition, seeing and living a compassionate lifestyle by working with those less fortunate is a part of being human that we should all strive for. By teaching yourself compassion and selflessness, it gets you to a point where you can practice it without thinking and as part of your life.
8. Recognize peak experiences: Along your journey, you will have transcendent moments where you feel something unique. These are sometimes called "peak experiences," as they represent you reaching a new peak along your path. Try to see them when they happen, or reflect back on times when you think you may have had one (Davis, 2019).
9. Be an honest person: Being honest and taking accountability for one's own actions seems like something most people do, but not always. Even if you are an honest person, you may not always behave like one. An example would be if you are upset about something and you exaggerate your point to make sure you are seen as right. Being

able to be accountable for one's own actions, and be humble about your mistakes is very enlightening and beneficial to someone on the path to self-actualization (Davis, 2019).

10. Take care of yourself: As we move up the levels of Maslow's hierarchy, your needs become less about the physical, and more about your esteem and emotional. But remember if one of the lower levels falls apart, then you don't have a solid foundation to work from. So make sure to keep yourself healthy, sleep well, eat good foods, and keep yourself in good physical condition.
11. Set goals: I could talk about goal setting endlessly. Being able to set goals and achieve them is something so special. Each one of us has our own unique vision of what we want our lives to look like and the goals to get there. The goal setting process can be part of your self-actualization. If you find the task of approaching your weaknesses a little overwhelming, take it slow. Make the goal to approach one each week. Then you only have to write one thing down that week and take the time to think about how it affects you and how you want to either accept it or change it. Only having to think about one new one each week is much more manageable then writing them all down at once.
12. Live a life of gratitude: I already mentioned how I wrote a list of my favorite things, and although there is some crossover, I also make lists of things I am grateful for. I'm grateful for my life, the food I am nourished with, my access to medical care, my family, and my home. I try every day to notice things in my life that are

extra special that I need to appreciate and be grateful for.
13. Remove negativity: This might be something that you do when you are trying to meet your self-esteem needs, before you even start on self-actualization. But it's worth saying again because if you can easily remove something negative in your life, then do it. I can't tell you how many times I've said that I want to get off social media because it doesn't bring light to my life, but I've always hesitated. Don't hesitate to eliminate things in your life that are unnecessarily bringing you down.
14. Smile: Seems simple enough, but just smile as often as you can. It might even feel slightly forced at first, but it will turn into something beautiful, I promise. I sometimes try having smile days. I smile at anyone within a five foot radius, and sometimes people look at me blankly, and other times I see their faces light up and I know I've made a small connection which makes me feel great.
15. Accept spirituality: To connect with a higher power of any kind can bring a light to your life, and a bond to work towards. It can bring you purpose and direction through your beliefs. It can give you a compass that centers you.
16. Don't wait for someone else: Remember that your path to self-actualization and mastering your thoughts is your journey. No one else is going to do it for you, or start the process for you. The only person that will push you and guide you to self-actualization and continue to keep you there is you!
17. Find your inspiration and your motivation: it can be exhausting when you are trying to analyze

yourself, and complete a journey to self-actualization. You need a light that you are working towards. Find what your guiding light is and use it to motivate you to keep going.

As you start your journey to self-actualization, remember that it's going to take time, and it doesn't end. Also remember that this is a beautiful process. If you are like me, even getting to a point where I had the ability to learn the word self-actualization was a huge accomplishment. Moving from a self-made mental hell as we discussed in Chapter 1, to a point of starting self-actualization was amazing for me.

I wanted to move through the first part of my process as quickly as humanly possible. I was so tired of being unhappy, negative, self-doubting, and just a shell of what I knew I could be. If we remember the hierarchy there are the five levels, and I didn't know if I would ever have a chance to move past level three. And level five seemed like something else entirely. A world I couldn't belong to. So once I felt like I had achieved level four, I wanted to savor the process to get to move to level five. I enjoyed, and continue to enjoy the process of getting to know myself and everything that's special and beautiful about me.

DETACHMENT: TAKE THE BY-PASS ROUTE AND ESCAPE THE BUSY FREEWAY OF YOUR MIND

Being able to detach yourself when you need to is a skill that I did not possess, and still struggle with quite a bit. I have a busy mind and I love to analyze things. If left to my own devices, I will think about things, and then rethink about those same things, and then do it ten more times. So learning how to detach has been incredibly challenging, yet probably one of the most valuable and rewarding skills I have gained.

Detachment is the ability to remove yourself from a situation, the thoughts associated with it, and the emotions that tie you to it. An example would be if you are really upset with an argument over a misunderstanding with a friend. You keep thinking about what you could have said differently, or how you could have communicated better. The idea that a different outcome could have happened consumes you. Detaching is being able to let go. You can let go of all the emotions and thoughts that you have built up about the situation and either deal with it or move on.

LIVING IN THE MOMENT

Part of detaching is being able to live in the moment. When I say living in the moment, I mean living your life so that you enjoy what's happening right now. You aren't stuck on things that have happened in the past, or things that may happen in the future. Instead, you appreciate everything that is happening as you exist in this time.

When we talk about negative thought patterns, living out of the present, and all the emotional disorders that we can suffer from, they all tie together. I will demonstrate this with a personal example:

I had a job waiting tables in university. It was a really high-end restaurant and we would get a lot of very wealthy patrons. I had a lot of regulars, and dealt with mostly really nice people. Often, there would be one table each evening that was the exception. It would be either one person or a group that were rude, patronizing, and very disrespectful. After working there for four years, I had built up quite the list of stories of poorly behaved customers.

With my tendency to gravitate towards negative thinking, and no tool set to combat it, my regular thoughts would be that I would only focus on that one table each night. I would do all the 10 ways of negative thinking. I would magnify small things, I would personalize it, I would jump to conclusions, and overgeneralize. I would put my mental filter on the whole experience of being a server to focus on those negative interactions and how horrible the people were. In addition, I would rehash stories years later about these same customers. After I told the story, I would be left to replay that interaction in my head subconsciously and, again, rethink all the things I should have said.

In addition to focusing on the negative, and all the

thoughts that surrounded those interactions, it affected other aspects of my life. Because I spent so much of my precious energy thinking about people that I didn't need to, I started to dream about them. I would relive rude customers through my dreams! How invasive and awful is that? I would develop anxiety if I saw those customers come in again, and would worry endlessly that a new table would be mean or rude to me. It was so unhealthy, and so exhausting.

I look back at that period of my life now, and hang my head a little. How frustrating to think about why I didn't focus on the hundreds of amazing customers I had. I spent so much time living out of the moment, that I didn't enjoy working at that restaurant as much as I should have. The people that owned the restaurant were so lovely, the other employees were fun, and most of the clientele were awesome. If I had learned to detach and live more presently, I feel like my experience over those four years would have been very different.

As I've learned more and more about self-actualization, I realize that even me looking back at this time and having regret is unhealthy. I've learned to detach from the fact that I can't go back and change that time period, and now I can just look at it through a different lens. I can use it as a learning experience and cautionary tale of what I don't want to happen again. It's now a reflection for me to remember that I don't want to miss out on current experiences, and I need to remember that to appreciate my present.

YOU EGO: HOW IT'S INHIBITING YOUR THOUGHTS

If you have never heard the term "ego" before, it refers to how you perceive yourself. Chitra Reddy describes it as "the feeling inside you which makes you feel different and special from everyone else" (2015, para. 6).

Every single person in this world has an ego. Some are much bigger than others. Our egos are a part of us when we are born, and then shaped and molded through our experiences the same as every other part of our personalities. By the time we reach adulthood, our egos may have developed in a variety of different ways, and most of the time we aren't even aware of the role they play in our everyday lives.

Going back to my restaurant days example, the reason so many of my rude customers bothered me so much had nothing to do with them. They probably never thought of me again after they left the restaurant. It had to do with my ego. Something they did or said hurt my ego, and it led me to ruminate on what happened. I saw myself as more important in the situation than I actually was, so I made it about me when it wasn't. I remember one time a customer kept making snide comments about the menu. He did it over and over when I was at the table. He complained about the ingredients, the menu options, a spelling error, and the fact that we ran out of a particular item. He directed his rudeness at me because I worked there, but it had nothing to do with me. I didn't do the inventory, the menu planning, or the printing, but I still took it personally. If I had known how to detach myself from the situation, I would have recognized that he was annoyed with the restaurant, and it had nothing to do with me.

Our ego is responsible for a lot of issues in our everyday relationships and interactions. How often have you been put in a situation where it became more about you being right than actually reaching a resolution? Our ego is what makes it important to "win" an argument rather than resolve it.

How Do I Control My Ego?

The first step to ensuring that your ego isn't a source of problems is by knowing it exists and being aware of what yours looks like. Do you always feel like you are the smartest person in the room? Do you feel like you know more about most things than other people? Are you someone that doesn't listen very well because you are waiting for your chance to talk?

We naturally all have an ego. It's part of being human. We are each living our own story and part of that is focusing on ourselves and what makes us different. Earlier I asked you to make a list of all your strengths and what makes you unique. You need to recognize these special features about yourself and celebrate them. The turning point of when an ego changes from acceptable to problematic is when you start to think you are more special than everyone around you.

Thinking you are more special doesn't necessarily mean you think you are better than other people. That is definitely a feature of an inflated ego, but thinking you are special sometimes means that you think you play a bigger role in things than you actually do. If I go into a coffee shop every morning and feel that a particular employee doesn't like me I may start to focus on that. I anticipate that I will get poor service from her and replay the interaction that we have after I leave. I build a story in my head around how she doesn't like me for some fabricated reason. Over time it goes from me being annoyed while I'm in the coffee shop, to me thinking about her on my way to the coffee shop, to me anxiously forecasting her mood while I'm getting ready in the morning. These spiraling OCD thoughts make me think that she is actively thinking about the ways she can be rude to me. In actuality, she doesn't even know who I am. She's never noticed our interactions, and she's not the friendliest because she works three jobs trying to save enough money to go to school. Her story has nothing to do with me, but my ego made me think I played a role in her life.

Your ego can consume your thoughts by making you worry about how others see you, and tricking you into thinking you are more important than you actually are. That's not me saying you aren't special or hugely important to a lot of people. It's me saying that you need to focus on the roles and places where you should focus your energy. On those days that I spent so much time fretting about the coffee shop employee, did I spend that same amount of time concerned about how my significant other and I interacted over breakfast? That's the person I should be spending my mental energy on, not a stranger who doesn't even remember me.

There are many ways to center yourself and keep your ego within a place you want it to be (Reddy, 2015):

1. Try not to take things too personally

This is absolutely easier said than done. If you are a sensitive soul like I am, you take everything personally. When something is eating away at me, one thing I have found valuable is to talk it over with someone I trust to get a new perspective. It can help me detach from the situation and remember that it may not be about me at all. One time a friend told me she was visiting her sick mom at the hospital. She was distracted and almost collided with another vehicle in the hospital parking lot. The other driver got out of his car and screamed at her for a couple of minutes. She was terrified by his extreme anger and the words he was saying to her. He then ran into his car and drove off. She said she'd sat there for a few minutes, crying. She was so scared and upset that someone would yell at her on a day where she was already so stressed about her mom. At that moment it dawned on her that he was leaving a hospital, and maybe he had just gone through something even worse than what she was experiencing. She realized his yelling at her had nothing to do with her and she let go of the situation and decided to be grateful that she could be the source for him to release some of his negative energy. What a beautiful way for her to look at it. She completely detached herself and chose to not take it personally at all. I really admired her for this.

1. Own your mistakes

We all make mistakes. I'm pretty sure I've made 10 today and it's only lunchtime! Keeping your ego in check involves accepting responsibility for your mistakes. If you do something wrong, even if you don't want to admit it, you have to be humble and acknowledge that it happened. This can be harder in some situations than others, but it's crucial on your path to self-actualization. The ability to put your ego aside and admit you made a mistake is nothing short of amazing.

1. It's okay to look foolish

Being afraid to look ridiculous, foolish, or stupid can sometimes prevent people from trying things or admitting things that they've done. In a world where we are expected to present the perfect version of ourselves, everyone is afraid to look silly and be judged. It can be scary to put yourself out there and get laughed at or be seen as ignorant about something. Just remember that being able to laugh at yourself and be silly is seen as very endearing. Think about the last time you saw somebody do something silly and have a good time doing it. Or someone who was brave enough to ask a question that might be looked at as dumb. You probably didn't judge them, and mostly likely appreciated them a bit more for doing so.

1. Remember that your ego is a part of you

It will never go away, even if you are the most humble person in the world. We can't help it. But you can be proud of yourself for trying to achieve a level of self-awareness about it, and for continuing to do so in the future.

1. Acknowledge your limitations

When we look back at when we wrote down our strengths and weaknesses. Being aware of what those are is part of being graceful and humble in our everyday lives. If I wrote down one of my weaknesses as being afraid to look silly, then I can acknowledge that and try to work on it. Before, I might have put one of my strengths as communicating with other people. Now, after learning what ego is, I realize that maybe I'm just good at talking about myself. That's okay because now I can be aware of it. I can try and talk about myself less, and truly become a good communicator by learning to listen as well. Everything we are working on ties together for the same outcome and is a continual process.

1. Focus on others

Since our ego is about us, what we think of ourselves, and how we feel about ourselves, just try thinking and focusing on other people. Give compliments, ask lots of questions about other peoples' lives and talk about other peoples' interests. When you are first starting out and trying to think about what your ego is and how it exists in your life, be aware of these things as you are talking to other people:

1. How often do you take over the conversation?

2. When someone is telling a personal story, do you quickly tell one of your own just like it?
3. Do you ask a lot of questions about other people?
4. Do you remember details from your last conversation?
5. When you leave the conversation, have you learned more about other people in the room, or are you more focused on how you came across during the interaction?

All of the above suggestions are meant to help you learn about your ego and how it plays a role in your everyday life. Being aware of it and how it affects your thoughts and interactions is the key way to not letting it consume you. Becoming wrapped up in our own thoughts, our self-importance, and just becoming overall self-absorbed is a very difficult way to live. It doesn't leave you open to learning from other people or really experiencing new things. Learning to control our ego is a way to prevent us from losing out on a whole different world.

DAILY TIPS TO FREE YOUR BUSY MIND, CONTROL YOUR EGO, AND DETACH WHEN NECESSARY

With all of this new information, I hope you feel ready to take on your life with a new zest and appreciation for the world outside of yourself. I want you to keep that excitement and that intentional self-awareness as you move forward in life. Trying to move past our own thoughts and think beyond our own needs is a lifelong process. It's something we all need to continually work on. Below are a few techniques I have discovered to stay true to this path:

1. Journaling

I know I say journaling a lot, but it really is a gift to me. Being able to write down my thoughts has been cathartic for me in ways that other techniques haven't. For you, it might be dictation of your thoughts through an app on your phone if you don't like writing, or maybe building vision boards, or bullet points on a whiteboard in your office. Detaching and freeing my mind through journaling enables me to dump my thoughts out onto paper and not look at them for a few days. That's how it helps me with detaching myself from a problem. When it comes to helping me with my ego, it allows me to look at how I approached a situation once I've had a few days to remove emotion. I can more easily identify how my ego played a role in my perception of a situation.

1. Setting an Intention

I like to set intentions for myself on a daily basis. I may have the same intention everyday for a month, or sometimes longer. If I find that I am having trouble letting go of things, or looking beyond myself, I will set an intention in the morning and say it to myself in the mirror. An example would be: "Today I am going to make someone's day better." I choose an intention like this to encourage myself to think beyond my own life. I want to put my ego, attachments, and emotions aside so that I can be better for someone else. That's a great way to clear my mind and be a small light for someone else who might need it.

1. Admitting a mistake

If it's not in your nature to point out your own flaws or errors, it might be very daunting at first. I am a very nonconfrontational person, so admitting a mistake has always been difficult—not so much because I don't like being wrong, but more so because I worry about how someone might respond. This is me making it about myself. A great example would be if you are having a really bad day and you are rude to someone who was trying to help you. It would probably be way easier to brush it off and not acknowledge that your behavior was bad because everyone has bad moods right? Just think how much better it would feel for you and the other person if you took the time to go and apologize for how you treated them and recognized that it wasn't fair.

1. Meditate

We've talked about meditation already, and I will go over more techniques in Chapter 10, but using meditation as a daily practice is as beneficial to me as journaling. Meditating will become your safe place where you can go over your thoughts with no judgement. You will learn to contemplate things patiently and remove the emotion and anxiety around topics and objectively approach thoughts without ego or attachment.

Going over the topic of ego can be difficult because we may feel like we are being reprimanded for thinking we are special or focusing on ourselves. I want to clarify and emphasize that it's not the case. You are a unique individual that isn't like anyone else on this planet. All the things that make up your personality make you special.

With the lessons involving ego we are trying to accomplish your self-actualization by understanding that although you are unique, you aren't the most important person in the world to everyone around you. As well, that you can't let a sense of self-importance cause your thoughts to spiral into negative places, or cause you to attach yourself to situations that don't concern you.

Ego can also sometimes prevent you from finding happiness because it can cause you emotions such as jealousy, sadness, anger, frustration, or disappointment. By becoming self-aware of your ego, and learning to put it aside when needed, you can free yourself of creating these emotions when you don't need to.

5

DETACHMENT FROM WHAT NO LONGER SERVES YOU

After covering what detachment is, and tactics to do it, the next thing is to learn how to identify when you need to detach yourself. In some situations, it's very clear and there's no question. Other times it can be a lot more difficult. Detaching yourself from complicated childhood experiences, personal relationships, or seemingly harmless situations are not as clear cut.

So how do you go about identifying things in your life that are creating you a lot of emotional harm? And when you do identify what they are, what are the different ways to approach them? We will talk about all these steps throughout this chapter.

I want you to practice setting an intention with this chapter. It can be very difficult to acknowledge that you have people or things in your life that are detrimental to you. It's a lot easier to think that this doesn't apply to you. Nobody wants to admit that a friend might be toxic, or that they are harboring hurtful memories about people that they love. So set the intention for yourself that you will read this chapter slowly and give yourself the chance to accept the possibility that it applies to you.

IDENTIFYING NEGATIVE INFLUENCES IN YOUR LIFE

I have segmented negative influences into four categories:

1. Your Home

This may be surprising to some. Your home should be your sanctuary and a place of peace. When you look around your home, is that the feeling that you get? Do you feel calm, secure, peaceful, and relaxed in your home environment? If the answer is no, then you need to try and identify why. Is it someone that lives there (which is another source of negative influence), the home itself, or possibly the state of your home? Quite often it is cited that an organized home lends itself to an organized mind. Seeing your home as a possible negative influence can open you up to making changes to fixing that part of your life.

1. Your Career

In an ideal world, we would all work at our dream jobs, and make money through our passions. I will say though, I've known people who acquired their dream jobs and it didn't necessarily make them as happy as they thought it would. It was still work. So keeping that in mind, take an objective look at your job. If you see it as a possible negative influence, try to think about why. You may find yourself in a negative environment where there is a lot of negative energy, such as complaining. Another possibility is that you have toxic people that try to negatively affect those around them. The job itself could be incredibly stressful and emotionally draining for you. Try to recognize whether it's the job that is the negative influence, or if you just don't like the work itself. The importance of this is that if you love what you do, and can recognize that it's the environment that is creating a poor situation, then you can try and move onto another company where you can do the same thing. But if you really don't like the job itself, then maybe you need to look at changing your career options, if possible. If you can specifically identify what the negative influence is, then you can arm yourself with ways to approach the situation. When trying to identify if there is something about your job that is toxic, try to assess your feelings at work. If you notice that you start to get anxious or uncomfortable around certain people or events, try to analyze what it is you are feeling and why.

1. Your Relationships

Identifying people that are toxic or negative influences is tough. I've devoted more time to this later in the chapter. The important thing to recognize about people being a source of a negative influence is that there are a lot of different ways to deal with it. You don't have to automatically eliminate them from your life. There are a lot of steps you can do to help with relationships. Your emotional connection to another human being is something that you want to celebrate and foster as much as you can. Cutting people out can sometimes be the only answer, but we aren't there yet on an emotional level. If you are in any way physically in danger, then the relationship is toxic and you need to remove yourself from it. That moves out of your self-actualization needs, and puts you back on level two of Maslow's hierarchy because your safety is in jeopardy. I can't stress this enough that you are strong enough to leave a physically harmful situation and recognizing that it is negative, harmful, and extremely detrimental to you, is necessary.

1. How you spend your free time

When you aren't at your job, or spending time with those close to you, what do you do with your time? Where is your leisure spent? I can think of a dozen examples of people I know that spend their extra time doing things that cause them stress and anxiety. I have one friend who spends all of their free time trying to become a social media influencer. Online they look like they are living their dream life, but in person I see that they are miserable and overworked. They have become absorbed by the amount of followers they have, the comments people make about them, or their ability to stand out against other influencers. I have another friend who golfs to the point of frustration. You might think that sounds ridiculous, but let me explain. A long time ago, he was acknowledged as the best golfer that most people knew. He was constantly given recognition by people at work, friends, and family as being an "amazing golfer." It got to the point that it became synonymous with who he was. He loved golfing and everyone knew he was great at it. Unfortunately, he started to feel pressure to stay that good and fit that expectation. So now he golfs to keep up the skill level as opposed to enjoying it. It seems ridiculous, but his ego drives his need to do it. It doesn't apply to everyone, but just consider that how you choose to spend your free time can sometimes create a negative influence or source of emotional turmoil that you don't even realize.

Take some time and think about areas in your life that possibly might be a source of negative influence for you. Some of them can be very easily fixed, and other's need a more delicate approach. No matter what the outcome will eventually be, taking the time to identify what the sources might be is the first step on creating a plan to detach the areas that no longer serve you on your path to self-actualization.

YOUR OPTIONS TO APPROACHING NEGATIVE INFLUENCES

At this point, you might have made yourself a list of negative influences in your life. Now what do you do with them? The answer is simple: Find a solution and fix it.

When it comes to your home and your job, it might be as simple as changing them. It can take courage to change something that is comfortable, even if it's a negative influence. If you recognize that one of these things has become a large source of negative energy and stress for you, think about how it will feel once you've moved on. Will you feel free and excited? Keep up your motivation for wanting to create this change. Be careful not to overwhelm yourself. Don't start a new job and move in a similar time frame. That can be a lot of change at once, and you want to make sure that each one is positive and puts you in a better place. You don't want to replace one source of stress with another.

When it comes to how you spend your free time and relationships, the methods to deal with them get a little more complicated sometimes.

With your free time, only you can decide if something you spend time on is worth the emotions it may create. When you think about things that you choose to spend your time on, just focus on this: Is it something that you need to do? For example, it might be hard on you, but if you regularly spend some of your free time helping a family member who relies on you, it wouldn't be easy to just stop helping them, nor would you want to. A different situation would be if you start out enjoying something but overtime it morphs into something that is more of an obligation (like my golf example). Do you have the ability to just stop doing it? Your time and energy is valuable. You probably spend a lot of time giving your energy to other people and activities, so try to engage in things that will fill that energy and life back into you.

When it comes to dealing with negative relationships, I look at the solution as a four part process.

Once you have identified someone in your life as a source of negative stress and emotion for you, ask yourself if they are a forever person in your life. What I mean by this is to evaluate how close they are to you. You're more likely to put more time and energy into your relationship with your mom than that coworker you only see on breaks. Another way to look at it is: Will you know this person a year from now? If the answer is no, then my tactic would be to avoid them and move on. Detach yourself from the relationship, and don't put a huge amount of energy into fixing something that is temporary. You don't need to create hurt feelings or anxiety for yourself or the other person if you see them as a source of negativity, but you know you will only have small interactions with them for a few months. Just do your best to place distance between you and engage in short interactions. If the person is someone that is with you for a long time, then you need a different approach.

For your long-term relationships, your next step is to identify the source within the person that is creating emotional distress for you. Are they constantly complaining? Do they tend to put you down? What is it that is affecting you, and do you play a part in it? If you have a close friend that loves to talk about other people behind their back, think about your interactions with them. Do you do it too? Try to be the change in the interactions that you are hoping to see. The next time you are with that person, try to change the subject and be more positive to see if they follow your lead. It might be easier than you think to change the negative energy your relationship has grown into. If you try this out for a while and are still not getting any sort of change, you will have to move on to having a direct conversation.

Having a direct conversation might sound like your worst nightmare. Especially if you've never had that type of conversation with this person before. Being fully honest, in my past, this is usually where I would jump ship. Rather than having an awkward conversation, I would either continue to let the relationship affect me, or just pull away to the detriment of our closeness. I really don't recommend this tactic. I am still guilty of doing it. I can't even count the amount of close relationships that I have probably lost out on over the years because of my inability to move forward on this step. What I have learned from the times I've pushed myself to approach someone I love with this type of conversation is that you eventually come out the other side closer. I would recommend going in with some sort of game plan of what you are going to say. I tend to get turned around and then spend days afterwards analyzing all the ways I could have said things better. If you go into the conversation with a plan and an intention to not attack or hurt the person, and instead aim to help them understand how you are feeling, chances are it will go well and you will be so much happier in the long run.

Occasionally it can go in a different direction. The other person could feel hurt and respond in a negative way. They might not agree with your assessment, or even just dismiss it. If this happens, it's unfortunate but it leaves the door open for you to move onto the next step.

On the small chance that someone close to you is not receptive to your needs, changing your relationship can be tough. You may feel like you made things worse and you should have just left it alone. It may feel like that for a while, but I promise you it will improve over time. The person on the other side of the conversation heard you. They may not have been ready to hear what you said, but they will think about it over time and maybe come to the same conclusion you did in their own time. Or maybe they will never agree with you, but will understand why you need to set boundaries moving forward.

Setting Boundaries: Why It's Important and How to Do It Successfully

Setting boundaries is a completely natural and healthy request when it comes to your personal needs and well-being. Your focus is trying to get to a healthier and best version of yourself. You are trying to move from a place of darkness and pain to a place where you can enjoy the small things and embrace life at full force. You are trying to become a version of you that feels light with energy flowing through you on a daily basis. When I close my eyes and see that version of myself I get so excited. I am so much closer to that person than I was a year ago, and I will be even closer a year from now.

The problem with the road to self-actualization is that not everyone is going to join you along the way, or be happy for you. Someone who isn't aware of their ego, or isn't in a place in their life to welcome growth, might see your success as their failure and want to get in your way. They might be negative, hurtful, or just not connect with you the way they did before. When it comes to these situations, you will go through the four steps we just talked about, and get to the point with some people that you just need to put up boundaries. You love them, and you always want them in your life, but you just need to protect yourself from their energy for the time being.

Boundaries can be defined as both physical and emotional. With each individual that you need to set boundaries with, you need to decide what boundaries are needed to protect both your relationship and your individual needs. Next, we will go over some examples of small boundaries that can be effective.

One step you can take is to request some time apart without fearing judgement from others. Let's say that you have lunch with your sister every week. You have identified that your lunches and conversations are a negative influence for you and you have the difficult conversation to which she laughed and brushed you off. You can set the boundary by saying that you understand that she doesn't see this as a big deal, but you do, and say that you want to take a break for a while from your lunches and you need them to be okay with it. Chances are they will be hurt but they will respect your boundary and possibly take your concern more seriously.

It is important to have the courage to say no. If you mustered up the courage to tell someone you love that they are hurting you and they were not receptive, then you can protect yourself by saying no to them for a while. When they ask you for your time or energy, decline. Reassure them that you are always available for emergencies and if they really need you, but for favors and free time, you need to say no for a while. You aren't punishing them for not changing, you are just allowing yourself the freedom to work on your own needs for some time.

Learn to speak up or remove yourself when someone's behavior is negatively affecting you. If you have a conversation with a coworker that is affecting your work space and they enjoy gossiping about other people around the office, then they might apologize and promise they will be more aware of it moving forward. Then a few weeks later, they slip into old habits and start right back into the same types of interactions with you again. Don't let your intentions slide, and be sure to remind them that it makes you uncomfortable, or remove yourself from the situation so you aren't an available recipient for them.

These are just a few examples of ways that you can be clear about what you need and what your expectations are from the other person you are struggling with. Remember that the only reason you are setting the boundaries is because you want to maintain the closeness of your relationship while still protecting your needs. You love and care about this person, and the boundaries are not meant to hurt or punish them. Make sure that they understand that and that you want their support. Being able to practice setting boundaries like this will become a lifelong skill that you can use for your own health and well being when you need it.

What if You Do Everything Right and They Are Still a Negative Influence?

If you have worked your way along the steps of trying to approach a negative influence and you are still left in a place of emotional turmoil with someone you love, you might just have to approach it from a different angle and create a permanent boundary. Josh Harbinger sites these seven toxic signs that it's time to cut someone out of your life (2018):

1. They ignore and don't respect your boundaries:
   You've tried to maintain the relationship by setting

boundaries to protect yourself from their toxic behavior but they disregard them.
2. They manipulate and control you: They use emotional tactics to control you. They can guilt you, cause you to doubt your decisions, and try to make you feel insecure to get what they want. They will do this without considering how it makes you feel.
3. They're dishonest: They don't think twice about lying to you to get what they want.
4. They will never admit when they're wrong: Dealing with a toxic person is a never ending battle that they are always trying to win. You've read threads of toxic people on social media arguing about the most ridiculous things. They argue to the point of humiliation in the quest to be "right." There's no reasoning with a person like that.
5. They judge you: When you've tried to talk with them about your needs, and your boundaries, they don't support you. Instead they judge you and try to make you feel bad about what you are trying to accomplish.
6. They play the victim: They will make you feel like you are abusing or mistreating them. That they are an innocent bystander in your attempt to be selfish. They will make this about them no matter how hard you try to explain what you need.
7. They take all they can, but never reciprocate: When you have that person in your life that continues to take all the energy you give them and never offers anything in return, even when you tell them that you need it, you may need to cut them off. They will forever be a drain on you, and you can't stay healthy and keep feeding into them.

If you have exhausted all of the ways that you can comfortably approach a negative and toxic relationship and you've identified them to be someone that you just can't hold onto anymore, you may have to remove them from your life. Gently.

Approach this process with two things in mind. You want to treat them with the same love and kindness that you would want them to treat you with. Even if they are cruel and toxic as you leave them behind, don't change your tone. Be kind no matter what. Set that intention and stay true to it.

The second thing is that the way you approach it will affect how you feel about yourself moving forward as well. If you lose sight of your intention and get pulled into an ugly argument, you will set yourself back on your journey. Use the skills you have been learning to be compassionate, patient, and self-aware as you separate yourself. You will grow as a result of this uncomfortable experience.

When you make the decision to remove someone from your life, your process will be your own, but this guide can help:

- Ask them to meet you for a talk. Let them know that it's serious and that you want them to please come prepared for something big. You don't want to blindside them. They think they're meeting you for a casual meet up and you hit them with a big decision.
- Let them know it won't take long. Set the expectation that it will be a short conversation. Hashing out a long separation will not work, especially not with a toxic person.
- When they arrive, let them know in your own words that you love them, that you know they love you, but that you have grown in different

directions and you can't have them in their life right now. If you feel that you are going to want to say more, write it in a letter and leave it with them.
- Make sure to bring any items of theirs that you may have so that they aren't looking for reasons to contact you.
- Ask that they not put any mutual relationships in the middle. This can include family members, joint friendships, or even acquaintances.
- Remove them from all forms of social media and general contact.

This can and will be a really hard thing to do, but remember what your reasoning is. Also remember that you've done everything you can to hold onto this person without affecting your own development and health. You are not a bad person, and you are healing yourself. You are keeping yourself healthy for the relationships that deserve you. Focus your energy on these individuals and situations. This is where you can gain new energy and grow together. These are the people that are supportive and happy that you are making changes in yourself. You sometimes have to move through some of the negatives and approach it head on to come out the other side a lighter and brighter person.

6

EMOTIONAL INTELLIGENCE AND HEALING YOUR INNER CHILD

How familiar are you with the term emotional intelligence? An American psychologist named Daniel Goleman is a leading contributor in the popularizing of the term and he describes it as having five key elements ("Emotional Intelligence in Leadership," 2009):

1. Self-awareness
2. Self-regulation
3. Motivation
4. Empathy
5. Social skills

Becoming emotionally intelligent comes through exploring these five areas and learning to be your best self in regards to each one. You will see some overlap with what we discussed in regards to the five points of self-actualization. The five points are: self-awareness, emotional exploration, emotional awareness, highlighting strengths, and highlighting weaknesses. The biggest difference is that self-actualization really focuses on understanding your emotions and how you relate to other people. It also teaches you to understand other peoples' emotions.

Self-awareness: This is understanding your emotions and being able to process them so you can understand how they relate to other people. A great example of this is being able to understand when you are not in a receptive mood. If you can identify that you are not open to a productive conversation at work because of a bad mood, you can relay that to a coworker and ask if they could set up a meeting with you on a different day so you can give them your full focus. It's not always that easy. Still, even by being aware of your emotions on that day you can try to detach from them when making work decisions that don't involve your personal feelings.

Self-regulation: This is the concept of being able to regulate your actions and behaviors. Continuing on with the previous example, if you come to work in a bad mood after arguing with your partner and a night of little sleep, you can self-regulate to not take that anger out on undeserved coworkers. Instead, you can act professional and regulate your emotions.

Motivation: Emotional intelligence involves our inner drive to succeed and develop. The fact that you are reading this book and are working on your own development means that you already have motivation for continued growth! Goal setting is a topic that has already been discussed, but it is a valuable tool to mention again. It gives us drive and a sense of accomplishment that feeds motivation and helps us want to keep moving forward.

Empathy: When we are striving towards being emotionally intelligent and learning to think outside of ourselves through self-actualization, empathy becomes a skill you will hone. With your desire to help others and connect with your relationships in a positive way, you will want to feel compassion and kindness for their emotions. If you don't naturally read other peoples' emotions well, then ask them. Ask your friends and loved ones how they're feeling and let them know that you're working on becoming more empathetic. At work, try to practice reading other peoples' emotions and asking them questions so you can be helpful when they need it.

Social skills: When you are getting to the point where you are moving into a life of thinking about others, you want to be able to develop your relationships to the best version of itself as well.

WHY IS EMOTIONAL INTELLIGENCE VALUABLE?

Your ability to improve your emotional intelligence will weigh in on your mental and physical health the same way that your own thoughts do. When I was first starting out, I spent an endless amount of energy thinking about my interactions and how they affected me. I didn't always communicate effectively and really struggled to express my emotions and thoughts clearly. My thoughts were already spiraling and were compounded with anxiety over the fact that I didn't come away from my interactions with other people feeling positive all the time. I was quite often confused. In addition, I would sometimes be embarrassed because I realized I was so focused on myself that I didn't always ask enough questions about them or what they were feeling and experiencing.

Your emotional intelligence will aid in your work performance, your ability to gain closeness with relationships, and your overall mental health. Certain areas may come more naturally to you and you don't really have to work at them, while others will push your comfort zone. I mentioned earlier my resistance to confrontation. I have really needed to work on my ability to approach conflict and resolve successfully. My previous tactic has been avoidance, and it was very hard on my inner thoughts and emotions.

I continue to reiterate that all of these things are not an overnight process. There are so many aspects to work on, and they all intertwine. Your strengths and weaknesses when it comes to emotional intelligence are formed from both your personality and the experiences throughout your lifetime. You may have difficulty with certain aspects because you had formative situations that happened when you were younger that also need time and development to lead you to a point where you can improve your emotional connections with other people. This leads me to the topic of your inner child.

WHAT IS YOUR INNER CHILD SAYING?

When referring to your inner child, people interpret in a few different ways. Some people look at it as a concept that every mature adult has a child within that wants to be carefree and released from the responsibilities of adulthood. For others it's the reflection of themselves as a child, and specific experiences that shaped them into who they are. And finally, there are some that look at their inner child as an accumulation of all their experiences and how they play into who they are today. Realistically, I think you have to approach your inner child as all three.

When I first heard the term "Inner Child," I didn't connect with it. I had a very happy childhood, and I assumed it was going to be a development process for someone who didn't have the happiest upbringing. I thought it would relate more to traumatic experiences, and the healing that needs to come with it. I was both right and wrong.

Your inner child needs may two things:

1. Healing from specific events
2. Recognition of its experiences and how they make you who you are

Healing from a traumatic experience is not something I am qualified to guide you through. The pain, suffering, and trauma that is associated with some events during childhood need delicate and thoughtful healing with the assistance of a professional. Speaking to a therapist or someone else that you trust to help you come to terms with such an event will enable you to accept that it happened, and let your inner child start to heal from its effect. It may potentially always be a part of you, but learning to accept it will help free you of the negative and emotional turmoil that it put you through.

The other part of addressing your inner child is recognizing both the good and the bad things in your childhood that formed you into the person you are right now. This can also help you understand why you feel certain things, communicate with people certain ways, or even get triggered by certain behaviors. When I say trigger, I mean you react strongly in a way that you don't always understand. A mild example would be if you get really upset with friends that are always late. You get very frustrated and overly upset about people doing this, but when you were a child, your parents were very strict about punctuality and found it disrespectful if you were late. A stronger, second example would be if you have a trigger from childhood trauma. If you had a parent that struggled with alcoholism, you may react very strongly to overly intoxicated friends. It's something that has been formed into you. That is a small trigger. Larger and more explosive triggers can also exist which were formed from more serious situations.

When you were a child you thought certain things, dreamed about your future, and found joy from places you might not anymore. Getting in touch with that part of you is really magical on your path to self-actualization. Imagine my "peak" moment when I realized that I am so afraid of conflict because I realized I was the peacemaker when I was a child.

Being the third out of four kids, I was constantly trying to diffuse sibling arguments and fighting when my parents weren't around. I then did that same tactic in school where I tried to be peaceful and friendly to everyone to avoid conflict and becoming a target of bullying. I can close my eyes and feel my younger self being terrified of people's attention and, even worse, the focus of their negative feelings. This was really enlightening for me to realize because it made me realize that I never developed any sort of conflict resolution experiences or tools because I avoided it at all costs from a very young age.

The final thing about your inner child that I want to focus on is inspiration. Remember that this whole road you are traveling is meant to get yourself to the version of you that your inner child wanted to be. Think about that for a moment. That's really powerful. When you were young, I guarantee you didn't dream about the day you could grow up and be trapped in a jail of negativity, anxiety, and distress, surrounded by toxic people and struggling to enjoy your life. That's not the version of yourself that younger you ever imagined would exist. Think back to what they thought they could be and all the things they knew they would achieve. Stay in touch with that inner part of you to remember that you are working to honor the way you anticipated your life to be. You deserve that.

DEALING WITH TRIGGERS

A trigger is a complex emotional response that needs its own set of tools to be dealt with successfully. As far down the road as you come and go on towards self-actualization, a trigger will throw you into a different spot without warning.

Let me give you an example of what I mean. Let's say you have been focusing a lot of your energy on addressing and managing your ego. You know that you tend to focus too much on your role in situations when in actuality, you don't have much of a role at all. You are sensitive and make things about you a little too much. You've recognized it, you're aware of it, and you are working on changing. You are doing fantastic. Then your closest friend tells you that they are moving to another city in a month. Your immediate thought is that they are abandoning you. One of your parents left when you were young and your friend moving triggers your fear of abandonment. In your head you know that their move has nothing to do with you, but because of your trigger, your ego wins and you make it all about you and your needs. You feel angry, hurt, disappointed, and confused, when you should be feeling happy for your friend who is excited about their move. It can be frustrating because you feel set back on your journey and don't know how to handle this type of reaction.

Identifying a trigger can be pretty easy, and you may be aware of them already. Sometimes our triggers even become a source of good-natured ridicule because our emotional response is so disproportionate to the trigger itself. Maybe you become really angry when you are really hungry and it's amusing to people that you spend a lot of time with. They tease you about it, but what they don't realize is that it's a trigger for you because you had an eating disorder when you were younger. Or it can be a smell of a certain type of food that made you really sick once, and now it triggers a physical response of nausea. Triggers present themselves in a lot of different forms.

If you have a trigger that you have identified as something that is serious enough to be impeding your ability to grow emotionally, there are a number of tips to help approach them. David Ricoh PhD discusses his "trigger toolbox" containing a variety of tips to approach triggers and deal with them successfully (2020):

1. Identifying and labeling them: Giving your trigger a name helps make it real and gives you a tangible thing to focus on. If my trigger is rejection, if I say it out loud to myself that I am triggered by rejection. It can help me realize why I am so upset when something small happens, like a friend bailing on me.
2. Try to remember why: Knowing the source of your trigger can help you lessen its power. If my rejection trigger comes from an awful break up when I was a young, then I can put into perspective that those were the actions of a teenager that caused those emotions in me. This enables me to heal.
3. Be aware of who you are punishing: It can be easy to project past experiences onto new people. Let's say you had a teacher that was verbally abusive to you when you were in grade school. The emotional scarring stayed with you and you have found it to be a trigger when your own children are attending school. If a teacher disciplines them or raises their voice, you get extremely defensive and overreact with anger. Try to be aware of when you are putting your own triggers onto people who don't deserve it.
4. Stay calm: If you notice yourself having a physical reaction to a trigger, employ your calming techniques, such as meditation, to bring your physical state back to a neutral place.
5. Listen to your inner voice: If you are triggered and there is something inside of you telling you something, don't disagree or push the feelings away. Acknowledge them and try to understand

why you are feeling them as opposed to dismissing them as invalid.
6. Show your emotion: When Dr. Ricoh discusses displaying your emotion, he likens them to a healthy development of any muscle. If you practice displaying your emotion regularly, your ability will become stronger. It's the same as if you use a muscle regularly. If you don't practice an emotion, such as sadness or anger, and mask them instead, then when they do come out, it will be difficult to control how you display them.
7. Step away: If the trigger is not something you feel capable of addressing when it happens, remove yourself from the situation. Promise yourself that you will come back to it when you are stronger. Don't avoid it forever, but give yourself space if you need it.
8. Laugh: If you are able to change a situation from a trigger to something you can find humor in, you've won and taken away its power.

Finding a way to respond to your triggers takes their power away and allows you to control the response that you have to them. As always, be patient with yourself and don't get frustrated if you slide into comfortable behaviors and react the next time something happens. Just remember that you are moving in an upwards direction to your self-actualized and emotionally intelligent self. Everything you are doing is providing you with the tools and weapons you need to eliminate the past behaviors and emotional disorders that have haunted you. EFT tapping is by far the most effective way to demolish your triggers in record time. It's free, easy to do, only takes a few minutes, and there are countless free videos online you can tap along to.

7

THE BEAUTY OF SELF-FORGIVENESS, SELF-COMPASSION, AND SELF-LOVE

As you have gone through this process, there have probably been some really tough moments for you. And you may be exhausted. You've been in a constant state of improvement, and trying to change. That takes a lot of work and a lot of effort. I want to devote some time for you to concentrate on what an amazing being you are. You need to spend some time falling in love with who you are and everything you have accomplished on this journey. You are incredible.

Over the past weeks, months, or years that you have been focusing your energy on this path, you have probably also had moments where you've been really hard on yourself. You might have been frustrated over things that you can't control. The negative self-talk can come out in full force when you are shining a light on all the things that you want to grow away from. This is the time where we are going to practice some compassion with ourselves and forgiveness for our past.

SELF-FORGIVENESS: LET THE HEALING BEGIN

We have spent a lot of time healing. We have focused on healing our inner child and our wounds from past experiences. We have talked about healing from toxic relationships and emotional connections. You have analyzed your entire soul, and all the flaws that come with it. And now is the time to forgive yourself for all the things that came before.

I reflect back on my story about my time working as a server and how much I missed out on because I couldn't see the beauty of everything around me. I missed out on friendships, interesting connections with customers, and probably unique life experiences because I was so focused on the negatives. I was really mad at myself for a long time afterwards. Then, as I began to move into a more positive version of myself, I got mad all over again. I held onto so much regret on how different it could have been.

Then I stopped to think: Why was I still beating myself up over this? What good intention was I bringing to my life by reflecting on things that happened years prior with regret, shame, and guilt? I needed to forgive myself for this experience and countless others so I could fully open myself up to new ones. If I reflected back on what an "idiot" I was for wrecking that time in my life, every time I had a great night out in a restaurant and enjoyed the atmosphere and the service, then there would always be a stain on the evening in my mind. Why would I want to do that to myself? I had to find a way to forgive my former self, and release my mind of the things that didn't matter anymore.

Exercises for Self-Forgiveness

- Write a letter: By now you probably see that I am a very big advocate of putting pen to paper to voice your feelings. Write yourself a letter the same way you would write a letter to another person to show them that you care. Tell yourself that you love you, and that you want everything good to happen for you in the future. You forgive your former self for anything that you wish you could change because it's over. The only one focusing on those things is you, and with your forgiveness, they are gone.

- Recite affirmations: Every morning (or when you have time alone), stare directly into your own eyes in the mirror and confidently recite an affirmation of forgiveness. This will be personal to you, but examples could be:
- "I love you and I forgive you for the past. You did what you thought was right, and everyone makes mistakes."
- "I forgive you. You are amazing. You are older, wiser, and forgiveness sets you free"
- Recognize the good that has come out of it: There will be things in your past that have bothered you that need forgiving. Reminding myself of good outcomes that have resulted from them helps me forgive myself for what's happened. I think about previous relationships that were ruined by my inability to connect in a positive way. My insecurities were able to take over because of negative self-talk and low self-esteem. These relationships hurt at the time, and I regret hurting other people, but the result was me finding a partner that I may not have met had the other relationships worked out. That's a positive thing. And my learned experiences from that other pain prepared me to appreciate the beauty of what I have now.

SELF-LOVE

You know what love feels like. You feel it towards other people. But have you ever stopped to direct that emotion inwards? Self-love is the practice of appreciating everything about yourself. It's taking the time to see yourself like other people do and love the things about yourself that they feel. Self-love is often overlooked because it's not a common concept. Even though it should be. You spend more time with yourself than any other person in the world, so why wouldn't you want to be in love with who you are?

Understandably, this may seem conflicting to what we talked about earlier with having an inflated ego. Being in love with yourself doesn't mean you think you are better and more important than everyone around you. It means that you can see the good in who you are and appreciate your inner beauty for what it is. So being in love with the special things about you doesn't have to mean that your ego is out of control. It means you know how to admire and cherish yourself.

Self-love also means taking care of yourself. It involves prioritizing your health and your needs to feel good about yourself. When life gets busy, taking time to look after ourselves is usually one of the first things that gets pushed to the side. We eat unhealthy foods because it's more convenient, we don't have time to stay fit, and we don't prioritize necessary relaxation. Sometimes we feel guilty and consider it selfish, but learning to detach from that thinking and show yourself self-care is necessary.

Exercises for Self-Love

- Physical care: Taking the time to nourish your body with physical care when you need it shows yourself a lot of love. Book a massage, go to a yoga class, take a nap, or partake in any other activity

where you put yourself first. Ask for support and promise yourself that you will always take care of your body when you feel it's necessary. You need to be able to rely on yourself to make those calls that your health will be a priority.
- Emotional breaks: As you go through a transition of personal development, things are going to get tough and you may want to quit. Be easy on yourself and take emotional breaks if you need to. Your mental health needs to be preserved, and even the strongest muscles need rest to get stronger.
- Disconnect: Turn off the screens, turn off your phone, and just enjoy time away from the overstimulating world we live in.
- Give yourself compliments: This may sound and feel a little silly, but it works! If I love someone, I want them to be happy. If they are feeling down, I like to cheer them up, or I like to make them feel good about themselves by giving them a compliment. So do it to yourself too. Look yourself in the eye and say something nice. "You did a really great job at work today," or "Wow! Your hair looks awesome." It's a bit cheesy but it will make you smile and fall in love with yourself a little bit more each time.

SELF-COMPASSION

I've used the phrases of being patient and kind to yourself as a theme throughout the chapters, and I sincerely mean it. We are so hard on ourselves every day. There's that saying "You are your own worst critic," and it's true! We are harder on ourselves than anybody else. So just lighten up every once in a while. We have big expectations of what we want to achieve, and putting pressure to reach our goals is a healthy attribute. But when the drive to do great things turns into negative self-talk when we have setbacks or failures, we need to show kindness to ourselves the way we would to anyone else.

Exercises for Self-Compassion

Dr. Kristen Neff is a leading expert in the area of self-compassion. She talks about practices for self-compassion (2019).

- Treating yourself the same way you would treat a friend
- Taking self-compassion breaks to make it a priority
- Writing and journaling
- Touch to calm and nourish your body and the parasympathetic system
- Moving away from negative self-talk
- Taking care of you and your caregiver

The one that resonated with me as the best way to show compassion to myself was to treat myself as a friend. For all my struggles with mental health and emotional turmoil, I can identify one of my strengths as being a good friend in a lot of ways. Definitely not a perfect friend, but I think a pretty good one. Flipping my thought process to treating myself the same way I treat my friends was really great for me. It helped me be very compassionate and kind to myself. I would never talk negatively to my friends the way I sometimes talked to myself. So why not show myself that same level of kindness?

So every once in a while, as an exercise in compassion to myself, I plan a day out. I pretend that I am planning a special day out for a friend the same way I would for their birthday. I pick my favorite restaurant for lunch, book a spa treatment, and organize meeting friends for drinks later. I show myself that I am special, and that I appreciate everything I'm capable of. I usually do this type of day at a time where I would normally be very hard on myself, like if I've had a setback or done something I regret. Showing myself compassion enables me to move on more quickly.

8

PUTTING YOURSELF FIRST IS NOT SELFISH

As we discussed the topics of showing yourself love, forgiveness, and compassion, the ability to be able to prioritize yourself was questioned. Many people have trouble putting time into themselves, and often feel guilty for trying to do so.

In some ways it can get a bit muddled, because on an ego level we put ourselves into the center of our thoughts, and in most situations we have to work on thinking beyond ourselves. In that context it sounds like we are putting ourselves first. Plus the fact that we are taking all this time to focus inwards and work towards self-actualization makes it sound like we are prioritizing ourselves. On some level it's true that you are learning to make time for yourself, but really being able to put yourself first is something almost entirely different.

In your life, you have people that depend on you. It could be children, a partner, friends, coworkers, elderly family, neighbors, and so on. It can be really hard to change expectations of your relationships when you have always been the person that is completely available and never says no. You enjoy being the one that a lot of people depend on, and you feel bad about setting aside time for yourself when you could be assisting someone else. Or you find it difficult to say no when something comes up and you already had something planned just for you. It can be really easy to tell yourself that you will reschedule your personal time, and then just help the person out who is asking at that moment. You don't prioritize yourself, and then it just becomes a habit.

LEARNING TO PRIORITIZE YOU

How do you go from being so busy and never saying no to setting boundaries and putting yourself first without guilt? It sounds like it should be simple, but something is preventing you from doing it already. Quite often we get into the habit of thinking we will have more time later, but later never comes. You just always stay busy and never learn to put you on a pedestal.

I mentioned earlier in the book that you need to have a source of light within you to keep the motivation of this process going. Your light comes from the source of wanting to be a better version of yourself. Our focus has been about you becoming this version for your own reasons. You want your life to be happier and healthier. When it comes to prioritizing yourself, it's important to remember that you are doing this journey for the people in your life too. By taking care of yourself, your mental health, and your physical being, you will be able to give more back to them and your relationship.

You should also look at it from an ego-less perspective. Are you feeling guilty about taking time for yourself because you believe everyone around you will fall apart because you are not available to be on call for them 24 hours a day? It sounds a bit silly when you put it in those terms. If you are a parent of very young children then it's probably not far off, but, even in that situation, being able to carve out at least 20 minutes a day to meditate or journal shouldn't be unreasonable.

Try these tips to begin the process of prioritizing your needs and detaching from the guilt that comes with it:

- Start small: If you feel guilty about taking time for yourself, work your way into it. Start with 20 minutes a few times each week. It can be as simple as turning your phone off, closing a door, and practicing mindful meditation.
- Ask for support: If you live in a home with other people, ask them to be respectful of your time. If you have children, ask your spouse to engage them while you have your time set aside so they don't come looking for you and interrupt you.
- Keep communication open: If putting yourself first is new, finding a balance of how much you need, and how much is too much can take awhile. If you have other obligations in your life, it might be difficult to go from no personal time to multiple hours of it a day. Keep communication open with those people in your life that may be affected. Ask them for support, but also ask them to be honest with their needs so they don't harbor any resentment if you are too absent.
- Think about what really matters: What would I do if I found out that I only had a month left on this Earth? Would I stress about all the little things that I am trying to accomplish instead of taking an hour out of my day for myself? No, I definitely wouldn't. It doesn't change the fact that I still need to get unimportant tasks done eventually, it just

helps remind me that they don't have to be done right at that moment. I can put them aside, and put me first.

DEFINING YOUR CORE VALUES

Your life is busy and you are trying to accomplish a lot with your development. You are learning to accept all the pieces of who you are, develop the weaker parts of your mind to free yourself from negativity, repair relationships, and focus on your own needs, all while learning emotional intelligence and removing negative influences from your life. You may feel pulled in many different directions, and even as you become better at prioritizing time for yourself, you may not always know how to maximize it.

Knowing your heart and what's in it will guide you to your purpose as a self-actualized person. Defining your core values will give you an inner guidance system that will help you with your decisions and help keep that inner light shining as you try to stay motivated and balanced.

Core values are the things in your life that you see as both important and necessary for your fulfillment and happiness. It's the values that you feel good about upholding and feel disappointed when you don't. They are the rules and influencers that you strive to live your life by.

There are hundreds of possibilities of what people's core values might be. Each one of us is so unique and what we hold in high regard might not have the same level of importance for someone else.

Some examples of popular values are:

1. Family: For many, their family is their main focus that drives them to be successful. Their family is their main priority because it is their primary social source and support system.
2. Achievement: Setting goals and achieving them is very important to someone who craves goal setting and reaching them. Achievement creates that inner sense of accomplishment and boosts esteem.
3. Structure: For some, having a structured schedule and being organized is calming and creates a positive environment that an unstructured environment does not.
4. Culture: Maintaining a connection to culture, family history, traditions, language, and community is very important. Preserving the culture by both practicing it and sharing it with family can be very valuable to people.
5. Laughter: Being able to laugh and find humor in everyday situations is a large priority for a lot of people who want to keep their spirit light and joyful.
6. Faith: For some, having faith is their compass for morality and finding purpose in life. Having faith provides many people with a sense of belonging and reasoning that is essential in their development.

7. Fitness: Prioritizing physical fitness is a source for many to alleviate emotional distress. It also creates a strong base to build upon.
8. Kindness: Being kind to people and treating everyone the same is a value held by many. This can mean stopping to think about others and reaching out to help when they need it.
9. Authenticity: Always being yourself. Never waver from who you are to fit other people's needs or expectations.
10. Giving Back - Being able to incorporate charity, community service, and other forms of giving back as a regular practice in life is very important to some people.

Writing down what your core values are can be a very interesting exercise. Maybe you've never put any thought into it before. Physically writing them down on paper could make you realize how important something is to you. I've always known that I enjoy creative projects, but it was only when I started writing down my values that I realized creativity is one of my core values. Not even just in an artistic sense, but also in how I approach problems and different situations. I value my creativity and use it to guide my decisions in many ways.

There isn't a correct number of values. You may have three, or you may have thirty. Think about what it is that you value and make a list for yourself so you can use it to guide you when you need it. It's also fun to go back years later and re-evaluate if your values have changed.

9

IT'S TIME TO REPROGRAM YOUR BRAIN

"Neuro-associations are the links between thoughts and emotions in your mind, which create and shape your behavior and performance results" (Girard, 2014, para. 7).

When you think about the potential of what a neuro-association is, and the abilities that we have to change them, the possibilities are endless on what we can train our minds to do. You have probably heard about simple neuro-association techniques like how chewing mint gum while studying for an exam will help you remember things if you chew that same gum later. Or maybe every time you hear a certain song it sparks a specific memory. These are all things that are associated through pathways in our minds.

We will have positive and negative associations. What we want to achieve is the ability to lessen the negative ones through neuro-association disrupting techniques and strengthen healthy ones through positive affirmations and other practices.

Liz Weighardt of the website *Happy Brain Life* discussed the example of how many people associate a dentist visit as a stressful experience and five tips to overcome that neuro-association (n.d.):

1. Find your "Why"

What is it specifically that you find stressful about the dentist? Using the calm and rational parts of your brain to try to figure out why you have this association can help you adjust and reprogram. If you had a bad experience when you were a child, you can acknowledge that it was in the past and unlikely to happen again. You can try and work on creating positive associations with the dentist now. Things like how clean your teeth feel afterwards or the sense of accomplishment you feel for taking care of yourself.

1. Understand your brain is just trying to help

Your brain isn't trying to make things difficult for you or even hurt you, it's trying to protect you. You have these associations because it's trying to protect you from having another negative experience. When you can think about it that way, it prevents you from being frustrated with your own mind. If you had a negative experience at the dentist when you were young, your brain is just trying to prevent you from having that pain again.

1. Use visualization

You can reprogram your brain with positive visualizations to create new associations in your brain. Since it only remembers the negative pain, try closing your eyes and visualizing positive images. Picture yourself relaxing in the chair, having a nice friendly dentist come in and greet you, and your beautiful smile when you are leaving. All happy, positive things.

Visualize them over and over for the days leading up to your appointment to strengthen that association and weaken the other one.

1. Positive Phrases

Talk positively to yourself about the dentist. Say phrases like "I love the dentist," "The dentist keeps me healthy," and "I am fortunate to have access to a dentist." These phrases will compound with the visualization to create better associations.

1. Tell your brain to stop

After you acknowledge why you have the negative association and what it is, ask your brain to stop. When you feel yourself drifting in that direction say "stop" to yourself, and move onto one of your positive association techniques. It won't be an immediate swap of associations, but over time it will change.

TECHNIQUES FOR RETRAINING

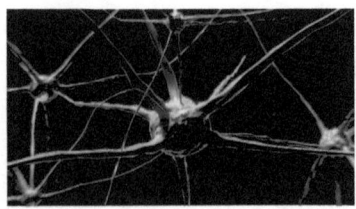

When I was young, I learned something in school about my brain. I remember a visual of pathways between connecting points in our brain. The visual showed a person thinking of something new and the pathway was a thin, tiny little line connecting to points within the brain. Then it showed them thinking about that same thing over and over, and each time they did the line or "pathway" got a little bit thicker. Then overtime, when they thought about that same thing enough, there was a thick bridge that was solid and unbreakable because it was so ingrained in their brain.

An example of this would be that 2+2=4. You have probably used that throughout your life thousands of times, so the pathway is so clear that you don't even need much energy to think about it. An example of a thin pathway would be a song that you heard when you were younger. Something reminds you of it one day but you have to think really hard about what it's called or what the tune is because the pathway isn't that strong and the line is thin.

I have no idea why this visual of our thought patterns stayed with me, but it was the first thing I thought of when I started to learn about neuro-associations. I panicked because I just kept picturing my negative associations as big thick lines that were strong and unbreakable. It was intimidating to think of how I could break them down and create new ones. What I did next has been my process for how I have changed my associations and have given new power to my mind and its abilities.

Visualization

We just spoke about visualizing with the dentist example. It is very powerful. This is how I used my pre-existing visual and started to use it to my advantage. I would label a negative association and picture it as a pathway in my brain. Let's use the example of vacation. Every time my family and I talked about going somewhere warm for vacation, my instant association was bathing suits and my poor body image. Basically it was an immediate association to "You're fat." How awful is that?

So through my visualization tactic I would:

1. Picture the pathway connecting two points in my brain with the writing on the side of the pathway as "vacation = you're fat."
2. I would then picture something coming and breaking the pathway. A rock flying right through the air and smashing it to pieces.
3. Afterwards, where the broken bridge was, I would picture my mind rebuilding the bridge with new writing. The writing would be what I wanted my brain to associate. In this situation the writing would now say "vacation = precious family time."
4. I would then picture a thought or an energy point traveling back and forth over the bridge to strengthen it and hardwire it into my system.
5. The next time I made the negative association, I would do it all over again.

Mindful Meditation

Coming back to our practice of mindful meditation, similar to its value with changing your thought process, it can be helped to reprogram your associations as well.

In our final chapters we will go over more techniques for mindful meditation and guided practices, but I often stick to a similar method to the one I discussed in Chapter 1. If you remember, I focused my mediation around breathing in the positive and pushing out the negative.

With respect to reprogramming an association, I use it in the same way.

- I breathe in the positive association that I would like to replace the negative one with.
- I breathe out the negative association and push it away from my body.

EFT Tapping

Our brief introduction to EFT tapping earlier gave a little insight into this exciting and life changing technique. I cannot say enough positive things about EFT, as it has become a regular source of relief and treatment for me in my everyday life.

I previously talked about my own methods for tapping, and introduced you to the various EFT points, and their connection to the meridians within our body. I would now like to talk more about the science behind how it affects our bodies and show you a guided technique for you to practice right away.

From a purely scientific approach, tapping affects your fight or flight response and disrupts the neural associations you've created. Your amygdala, which is the part of your brain said to be the core of your nervous system and the section responsible for our fear responses, is affected by the process of tapping. Brain scans have been said to show that the amygdala is directly affected during the tapping process. At this time, it's unclear the definitive changes that are happening, but the proof is in the thousands of people that are seeing results through its practice (Howitt, 2019).

Getting started on traditional tapping basics is not complicated:

- You will start your tapping process by creating a setup statement. We will go over the setup statement shortly.
- You repeat the setup statement slowly as you move through a sequence of tapping points, starting with the karate chop point. The entire sequence is listed below.
- You repeat the sequence over and over until you are able to let go of the negativity and harsh

emotion associated with your concern and come to a neutral place. Once you have cleared your mind of negativity, you are open to repeat the sequence with a more positive statement in mind.

With this explanation you can see how wonderfully uncomplicated and freeing it is. By tapping while repeating your setup statement, you calm your body and allow yourself to accept your intention stress free.

The setup statement mentioned is the statement that you will use to define what you are struggling with and your acceptance of it. It is basically your intention for your tapping session. In our dentist reprogramming example, your statement might be:

"I am afraid of the dentist, and that's okay."

"A dentist hurt me in the past, and I forgive him."

"The dentist office makes me anxious, and I accept that."

Your intention statement allows you to acknowledge your fear and negative association. Although there hasn't been enough testing, theoretically it could be said that by acknowledging our fears and negative associations we engage the fight or flight response of our amygdala. Then, by tapping through that it causes our brain to lessen the response to that particular stimulus. By lessening the negative association it sets us up to succeed in creating the more positive associations through our other techniques of meditation and visualization.

The sequence of your tapping points are as follows:

1. Start with the side of your hand. It's called the "karate chop point." Use the four fingers from your other hand and tap the spot on the side of your hand right below the bottom/outside part of your pinky. If you were to make a karate chop motion, it is the point on the outside of your hand that would

connect. Recite your Intention Statement three times slowly while tapping this point.
2. Next tap five to seven times on each of the following points while repeating a focused word out of your intention statement. In our example it would probably be "dentist." Start at the top of the head point and work your way down to the underarm.
3. Tap Top of Head 5-7 times (TH)
4. Eyebrow Point (EB)
5. Under Eye (UE)
6. Under Nose (UN)
7. Chin Point (CP)
8. Collarbone Point (CB)
9. Under Arm (UA)
10. Repeat the process until you feel in a neutral place with your fear and anxiety dissipated.

This now leaves your brain in a neutral place to begin creating positive associations towards your negative thoughts. At this point, I find the other techniques to be more powerful for myself for positive association creation. However, the same process of EFT tapping can be highly effective with positive associations.

When you start the process, make a positive intention statement:

"I will approach the dentist without fear."

"My health is the priority and I am appreciative."

"I am grateful that I have access to dental care."

Then follow the exact same process with the intent of creating a positive association.

SELF-DISCIPLINE

Moving forward, it's important to remember that these techniques are only as valuable as your resolve to use them. Their effectiveness will come through consistency and commitment. You can't reprogram a deep association with one session. It has to be an ongoing thing to strengthen what exists and build up what you want it to be.

In the beginning, don't try to reprogram every part of you that needs some change. It would be impossible both time-wise, and for your brain to take on. Chances are you don't have mass amounts of items that need to be reprogrammed, and certainly not many serious ones. Just pick one to start with. Even try something simple like a type of food.

This is actually how I practiced. For years I didn't eat a certain type of soup. I had become sick once after eating it, and every time I smelled it afterwards my stomach would do a little flip. Then as time went on, I didn't have the same physical response, but associated soup with feeling sick. I used this type of soup to practice my skills. I used all the techniques I had learned to reprogram my brain to remember that I used to like this soup and the flavors are all things I enjoy. Guess what, it worked! I don't have that association anymore, and I enjoy that soup again.

After my success with that, I was excited to move onto more reprogramming so it made it easier for me to commit to something I had actually seen work. Give yourself the gift of self-discipline to stick to these techniques. They can help you endlessly in your quest for self-actualization and ongoing growth.

AMAZING MEDITATION TECHNIQUES TO MASTER YOUR THOUGHTS

Meditation is a practice of calming your mind, emptying the clutter, and focusing your thoughts to a positive place. It is the one natural technique that has had extensive research and medical studies performed that prove the theory of its effectiveness. Studies have shown that it is responsible for physically changing your brain. Long-term meditators show less aging within their brain (this is displayed through gray matter volume). It decreases activity in the default mode network (DMN) section of your brain which is responsible for wandering thoughts. Those wandering thoughts in some cases are the negative, OCD, anxious, and depressing thoughts that lead to mental health issues and are associated with lower happiness. By reducing activity in this area, you are diminishing the presence of these thoughts. Through controlled testing, mediation is also shown to improve focus and concentration. Its benefits for your brain are nothing short of outstanding (Walton, 2015).

There is no correct or incorrect way to practice meditation, but there are endless resources of different ways to accomplish your intentions of what you would like to achieve. Testing out different methods will help you discover the most effective one for you. Below are some of my favorite techniques that I have found to be incredibly effective for me to reap the benefits of meditation.

TECHNIQUE 1: CONCENTRATION MEDITATION

Concentration meditation is the practice of focusing on one thought, idea, or object for an extended period of time. It's meant to teach you to focus more intensely. In the beginning, you may only be able to maintain your focus for a minute or two, but will work up your endurance over time.

For concentration meditation, since you are going to be focusing your thoughts and energy into one spot, you can choose to concentrate on the following:

1. An object: Many people choose objects that represent nature and make them feel grounded. A candle, to focus on the flicker of the flame. A stone. A flower or a plant. You can choose any type of object. It is something for you to place in one spot and focus on.
2. A phrase or word: You don't always have to use the same phrase or word. It can be changed day to day, depending on what you would like to concentrate on for that day's meditation. You can repeat it slowly as you learn to focus your energy into the one spot.
3. Your breath: I mentioned this earlier in the book that this is something that I focus on during my meditation. Breathing in and out slowly and focusing on the sound, feeling, and duration of each breath.

With concentration meditation do the following steps:

1. Pick a comfortable spot to start. Using the same spot every day can condition your body to associate meditation and its positive benefits to that place. This can create a very special place for you in your home. But also learning to meditate in a variety of places can be helpful to your commitment to it as well.
2. Decide the duration of your meditation practice and set an alarm. Pick a gentle alarm that will gently pull you from your meditation, rather than jolt you back to awareness.
3. When you are comfortable and ready to start, take a few deep breaths and concentrate on your object, words, or breath.
4. Continue to take deep breaths in and out while concentrating.
5. If your mind begins to wander, don't get frustrated. Feeling upset with yourself is also a distraction so don't let yourself get caught up in it. Just take a deep breath and push away distractions. Then, with your next breath, refocus back on your concentrating.
6. Lengthen your meditation over time. In the beginning, start with a few minutes, and then work your way up to 20-30 minutes.

Concentration meditation is very beneficial for teaching your mind to focus and spend less time with wandering and disruptive thoughts. It can help you in your everyday life ,at work or with relationships by giving you the skill of deeper focus.

TECHNIQUE 2: MINDFULNESS MEDITATION

We discussed mindfulness meditation earlier as it is my favorite form to practice. It's the tactic of giving your mind a safe space to allow various thoughts a judgement free zone to pass through. For someone who has had trouble with OCD and negative thoughts, I think it gives me the best ability to detach and let go of my wandering and troubling emotions.

I went over my technique in detail in Chapter 2. but to summarize:

1. Find a quiet, comfortable spot away from all distractions.
2. Relax into your spot. Make sure you are physically fully relaxed. If you are chilly, put a blanket on. You don't want physical distractions to take away from your time.
3. Slowly breath in and out to the count of five. Focus on your breath, and as thoughts enter your mind, acknowledge them without judgement or analysis. If a thought is something that you need to work through, breathe in the positive associated with the thought, and breathe out the negative.

Mindfulness meditation creates an escape for your busy mind to clear away negative thoughts and emotions. It gives you peace to know that you can go to a place to calm your emotions. For me, it took away my sense of powerlessness that I felt when I got stressed or upset. I didn't always know how to cope with it, but having a place that I know is waiting for me makes me feel safe and secure.

TECHNIQUE 3: WALKING MEDITATION

When you go for a walk, what do you think about? Even when you are walking from your car into a building, or walking around your house, where do your thoughts and focus go? If someone had asked me those questions a few years ago, I don't even know if I would have an answer. We tend to go on autopilot when we are walking, or we are busy thinking about things that need to get done.

Walking meditation is the practice of paying attention to your surroundings while walking, as well as using your natural walking rhythm as a method to maintain your focus. Similar to yoga, it uses the natural movement of your body to connect your breath, movement, and thoughts. In addition, if you are practicing walking meditation outside, you can connect your senses to the nature around you.

Perform this walking exercise as described from the online source *Headspace* ("Walking Meditation," 2020):

Do each of the following cues for about 30-60 seconds and then repeat from the beginning:

Body Check: Start at the top and sense your way down. How do you feel? Pay attention to any aches and pains, or points of tightness. Being aware of how your body feels can allow you to acknowledge your physical state. If you feel tired and heavy, then make feelings of lightness and energy part of your meditation as you walk. Adjust your posture to stand tall and feel strong.

Observe: Just pay attention to the way you walk. Maybe you've never noticed that you swing one arm way more than the other, or that your hips sway a lot. Don't try to change it, just enjoy your movement.

Tune in: Listen to everything that's going on around you. Listen to birds, music from passing cars, the wind, your footsteps, and anything else that catches your ear. Look at everything you pass in detail. Notice the bright color of flowers, interactions of people, the trees swaying, and other beautiful things you may normally have just sailed on by without noticing. Lastly, notice the smells. Breathe in the fresh air and anything else you can.

Physical Sensations: Notice the physical sensations as they happen. If it's cold, notice the wind on your cheeks. Feel the weight of your bag on your shoulder. Feel the tension in your legs. Enjoy the contact of your feet with the ground. Use these sensations to create awareness in your body.

Over time, I've created my own version of walking meditation that I call the five senses. I use each of the five sense on rotation to create a meditation sequence while I'm walking:

Taste: I always have water with me. I use a large sip of cold water as my centering and starting point to the sequence. It also provides me with a reset option if my mind has completely wandered off, or if my dog distracts me and I want to restart the process.

Sight: I take a few minutes to observe things around me and give gratitude to nature. I look at the sky and thank nature for clean air. I look at the flowers, trees, and grass, and thank nature for the healthy ground. If I am walking in the city, I observe people and give gratitude for kindness and compassion.

Smell: After sight, I take note of the smells, and connect as much as I can through familiarity of things I have smelled before.

Touch: I stop to touch something to feel more grounded. I will touch a tree, or a plant, or even stop to pet an animal. Something to engage my physical senses.

Hearing: I will listen to the sounds around me. I'm careful not to focus on words or conversations because then my mind will drift. Rather I try to find patterns in the sounds of the city of nature.

Once I'm done with the sequence, I start back to the beginning with a sip of water. The purpose of walking meditation is to maintain awareness of our bodies and our surroundings instead of passing it all by distraction in meaningless thoughts. It helps us stay present and enjoy the moment.

TECHNIQUE 4: CHAKRA MEDITATION

The ancient Buddhist practice of chakra meditation focuses on seven energy points along the spine. Each energy point has a specific point, name, and color associated with it. It is believed that if any of your chakras are "blocked," it prevents you from health and wellness associated with that point.

When practicing chakra meditation, you start with the lowest energy point and work your way upwards. By focusing on the point and visualizing the color associated with that chakra, you can work on realigning its energy to bring balance to your body.

The seven chakra points starting with the base and moving upwards are:

1. The root chakra (red color): Located at the base of the spine near your tailbone. A blocked root is associated with anxiousness of finance, basic needs, arthritis, constipation and bladder ailments. A balanced root brings feelings of stability, grounding, and calmness.
2. The sacral chakra (orange color): Located just below the belly button and above the pubic bone. A blocked sacral is associated with lack of creativity, sexual impotency, and urinary infections.

A balanced root brings creativity, sexual confidence, and self-worth.
3. The solar plexus chakra (yellow color): Located between the rib cage and the navel. A blocked plexus is associated with digestive issues such as ulcers and heartburn. A balanced root brings high self-esteem and confidence.
4. The heart chakra (green color): Located in the center of the chest. A blocked heart is associated with heart attacks, weight issues, selfishness, loneliness, and low self-esteem. A balanced root brings love, and the ability to communicate with others.
5. The throat chakra (blue color): Located directly in the throat. A blocked throat is associated with throat problems, dental issues, negative communication, and dishonesty. A balanced throat brings strong communication and a healthy smile.
6. The third eye chakra (indigo color): Located in the space between your eyebrows. A blocked third eye is associated with headaches, poor hearing, and foggy thinking. A balanced third eye brings clarity and imagination.
7. The crown chakra (deep purple): Located at the top of the head. A blocked crown can be associated with brain function and nervous system issues. Since it is connected to the entire body through the brain, it can affect all organs negatively. It is also associated with narrow minded and negative thinking. A balanced crown brings balance to the entire body, kindness, compassion, and intelligence.

To practice the chakra meditation, simple breathing and visualization techniques are effective. There are two methods:

1. Follow the seven chakra points from root to crown. Take slow, deep breaths while visualizing each point. Picture the associated color and breath into the energy point. Visualize your breath giving energy to the point and making the color brighter and full of energy. As you exhale, push out the negative energy manifesting itself in that energy point. Spend a few minutes on each point.
2. Concentrate on one chakra that you feel is out of alignment. For example, if you have been getting a lot of headaches and can't seem to focus, spend time on your third eye chakra to bring balance and alignment back.

Chakra meditation is a powerful method of bringing a sense of calm and alignment to the body. It can be used to compliment your other types of mediation by adding a unique and effective method of visualizing positivity into your various energy points.

Whatever your method of choice for meditation is, remember to be consistent and try to do it every day. The purpose is to create a clearer, healthier, and calmer version of your brain to help you with your journey to self-actualization. It's an extremely valuable tool and I am so grateful I am able to share it with you.

11

THE 10 STEP DAILY EMPOWERMENT RITUAL FOR MASTERY OF YOUR THOUGHTS

You have experienced so much growth during our time together. I hope you have learned everything that I have poured from my heart in the hope to help you grow. I feel so blessed in my life to have come across so many profound and wonderful people who share their wisdom with love and acceptance. I want you to feel that same level of support from me as you continue on your path.

I have spent years developing a routine that works for me on a day to day basis to maintain my ongoing commitment to self-actualization. Getting comfortable within my own skin and accepting every aspect of who I am has been the journey of a lifetime. I want to share my routine with you so that you have a starting point of creating the perfect life for yourself.

This routine is something I do each and every day. When I am struggling or going through some extra emotions, I will add time to the routine to get through everything I need to, but I will put my extra care tips in here as well. By keeping this routine up, I feel like my mind is lighter, more free, and clearer than it's ever been in my life.

MY 10 STEP SECRET ROUTINE FOR SUCCESS:

Step 1: Each evening before I go to sleep, I write a phrase or word on a chalkboard hanging by my bed. When I awake in the morning I look to the board and see what I have written. Some days it will be something specific for that day such as "You are brave, and your interview will go great." On other days it will be something I set as a general intention, like "Love freely today, show the world your heart." I used to wake up and reach for my phone. I would check emails and read the news, which set my mind racing for the day. Now I wake up calmly and with a great start.

Step 2: I take five minutes to stretch and breathe. I do a few stretches to wake up my body and get myself connected before I start my day. I reach to the sky and breathe in, and then reach to the ground as I breathe out. If you are familiar with sun salutations in yoga, it is a similar concept.

Step 3: As I get myself ready I say positive affirmations to myself in the mirror. Staring directly into your own eyes is a very powerful experience. I had never noticed it before, but I think I always avoided eye contact with myself before. I was always looking at my hair, or focused somewhere else on my face. It's a very different feeling when you stare deep into your own eyes and recite something positive. It makes you feel supported, strong and focused as you start your day.

Step 4: As I eat my breakfast, I write in my journal. I will write an intention for the day as well as something I am excited about or grateful for. It focuses my energy for the day to a positive place.

Step 5: I walk to work, or on my days off, I go for a recreational walk. I practice walking meditation.

Step 6: Throughout the day my time gets pulled in a lot of directions, and focusing inwards isn't my priority. To stay focused, I practice tapping at my desk one or two times each day to distract my mind from any negative thoughts or out of control emotions.

Step 7: Each day I have a goal to compliment three people. I make a point of creating conversation to improve my emotional intelligence by complimenting someone and creating a conversation around that compliment.

Step 8: Each day I set aside 10-15 minutes no matter what for meditation or visualization. Whether I am working through a specific goal of retraining a neuro-association, meditating over something that is bothering me, or practicing concentration meditation to improve my focus, I dedicate that time for my brain's health. This is my mental workout and I never miss it.

Step 9: At the end of the day I go back to my journal and write the three things I mentioned when we were talking about tips for self-actualization. I write one thing about my day that was great, one thing that I struggled with, and one thing that I observed that had nothing to do with me.

Step 10: I reflect on my day and decide to set my intention for the next day. I firmly believe that if I go to sleep visualizing the words I just wrote down for the next day, my mind marinates them all night, and the next day I live by them authentically. It's stunning to realize how much power our thoughts have to set the tone for a day full of experiences.

By following these ten steps each and every day, I have found myself to be happier, calmer, and emotionally healthier. The difference is so huge, I struggle to find words to display the difference between who I was and who I am now. I feel completely different, and approach life in an entirely different mindset.

Follow these 10 steps like I do, and make them your daily practice. You will feel empowered, free, and fully in control of your own thoughts and emotions.

AFTERWORD

When we started out on our journey together, I told you that you would learn more about your mind and its abilities than you ever thought possible. Your brain holds possibilities to give you the life you've always dreamed of.

When I started my path years ago, I didn't even realize I was in such a dark place. I genuinely thought I would lower my stress and increase my positivity and I would be fine. Even looking at that and seeing that my goal was to be "fine" is heartbreaking to me. I am so grateful that I came to know all these wonderful methods and knowledge that have enabled me to strive for more.

More is what I want for you too. I know that you are capable of great things. You too can connect to your emotions and master your thoughts. By doing this you will see benefits pop up in all different facets of your life.

STAYING YOU

The theme of mastering your thoughts and living a path to self-actualization is one of change and growth. But a concern that some may have is: Do you lose who you are along the way? Do you spend so much time trying to focus inward, that you forget who you are in relation to the rest of the world? Do you change so much that your connections with other people change and dissolve as a result?

We talked about finding and clarifying your core values. This will act as a guidance system so that you don't ever lose focus on who you are deep down. The point of self-actualization and growth is not to lose what makes you unique. Self-actualization is meant to accentuate your favorite and most positive parts of yourself, and cope with the negative and turmoiled parts you've been living with. None of this will change the things you laugh at, your favorite foods, or the way you smile. You will still be you, only a healthier and happier version.

Along the way, you might have relationships that don't like this version of you. There's the old saying "misery loves company." It's unfortunately true. If someone in your life is also unhappy, but not open to a new path, they may be angry at you for moving forward. They won't have the mental capacity at this time to be happy for you and your relationship may suffer.

Get excited about your future. You have now armed yourself with a toolbox bigger than most people on this planet have. You understand your thoughts and emotions with more awareness than most people you know. You have abilities to control your mind. Now remember how powerful your brain actually is, and think about how profound that is.

MY ENDING POINT

Do you remember my stories about my vacation, and the time I worked as a server? Do you remember my mindsets for each of these stories? Now listen to one that happened to me about a month ago.

Last month I was quickly running to the mall to grab a gift for a child's birthday party. I was in a rush leaving the house so I wasn't looking my best and I ran into someone that I worked with at that restaurant! What happened next for me was nothing short of a miracle. I was nothing but happy to see them. I excitedly told them about things happening in my life and eagerly asked about theirs. I genuinely enjoyed our interaction and walked away feeling energized.

What made me even more happy is what I would have done in that situation a few years earlier. I would have immediately been embarrassed about how I looked and been self-conscious the whole time. Now I didn't even care. I'm so much more confident that it didn't phase me. Plus my ego is smaller so I realized that they weren't super dressed up either and it didn't matter to me, so I know they would be thinking the same thing.

I would have been frantically trying to think of things going on in my life that they would care about and not listening to what they were saying. Or even worse, I might not have even asked because I was so self-absorbed. Now I genuinely have things I'm excited to share and really want to know about their accomplishments.

I would have been distracted trying to remember things that I had to get done, or worried that I wouldn't have enough time to get my errands done that I wouldn't have been very engaging. Now because I'm more focused, my schedule is better organized and I'm not always rushing and feeling frantic. I was able to relax and enjoy the conversation.

I would have walked away stressed about what they were thinking. I would have made up stories in my head about how they thought I looked heavy, or seemed rude, or any number

AFTERWORD

or negative thoughts. Now I walked away thinking how great it was to see them, and didn't put any thought into what they were thinking about me.

This small interaction was a peak moment for me. Look how far I had come and what I was able to do. I felt a sense of accomplishment walking away from that person that it almost brought me to tears. It was in that moment that I had my first inkling that I had reached some level of self-actualization. I know that the growth never stops, and I will continue to practice my 10 steps daily and work on other areas as well, but I felt pretty great that day. This is the peak moment that I want for you, and that you will experience over time.

Thank you for sharing your time with me and giving your energy to this book. Your devotion and passion towards yourself will create a new future for you. Remember to be kind to yourself, be patient, and enjoy the journey.

REFERENCES

All photos sourced from pixabay.com

American Psychiatric Association. (2008). "What is obsessive-compulsive disorder?" Psychiatry.org. www.psychiatry.org/patients-families/ocd/what-is-obsessive-compulsive-disorder.

Burns, David D M.D. (2008). Feeling good: The new mood therapy. Harper.

Davis, Matt. (2019, August 20). "8 ways to achieve self-actualization." Big Think. bigthink.com/personal-growth/achieving-self-actualization

"Emotional intelligence in leadership." (2009). Mindtools. www.mindtools.com/pages/article/newLDR_45.htm.

Girard, Joe. (2014, March 3). "3 ways to be memorable using neuro-associations." Joe Girard. joegirard.ca/neuro-associations/

Harbinger, Jordan. (2018, March 5). "7 signs it's time to cut a toxic person out of your life (and how to do it)." Jordan Harbinger. www.jordanharbinger.com/7-signs-its-time-to-cut-a-toxic-person-out-of-your-life-and-how-to-do-it/

Howitt, Nigel. (2019, February 6). "EFT (Tapping):

Healing through reprogramming the subconscious mind." Lawful Rebel. lawfulrebel.com/eft-tapping/

Kelly PhD, Owen. (2020, March 8). "Could an herbal remedy help relieve your OCD symptoms?" Verywell Mind. www.verywellmind.com/herbal-remedies-for-ocd-2510631.

Lyons, Deanna. (n.d.). "EFT handouts." Deanna Lyons. deannalyons.com/eft-handouts/

Mayo Clinic Staff. (2020, September 15). "Mindfulness Exercises." Mayo Clinic. www.mayoclinic.org/healthy-lifestyle/consumer-health/in-depth/mindfulness-exercises/art-20046356.

Molinoff, Mark. (n.d.). "Raleigh acupuncture obsessive compulsive disorder treatment." Raleigh Acupuncture Associates. raleighacupunctureinc.com/raleigh-acupuncture-obsessive-compulsive-disorder/.

Neff, Dr. Kristen. (2019). "Self-compassion exercises by Dr. Kristin Neff." Self-Compassion. self-compassion.org/category/exercises/.

Raypole, Crystal. (2020, February 27). "Self-actualization: What it is and how to achieve it." Healthline. www.healthline.com/health/self-actualization#characteristics.

Reddy, Chitra. (2015, October 14). "How to control your ego problems: 10 best tips." WiseStep. content.wisestep.com/control-ego-problems/.

Ricoh PhD, David. (2020, September 20). "13 strategies to deal with your emotional triggers." Experience Life. experiencelife.lifetime.life/article/13-strategies-to-deal-with-your-emotional-triggers/.

Selva, Joaquin. (2019, June 26). "What is self-actualization? A psychologist's definition [+ examples]." Positive Psychology. positivepsychology.com/self-actualization/.

"Tapping 101." (n.d.). The Tapping Solution. www.thetappingsolution.com/tapping-101/

"Walking meditation." (2020). Headspace. www.headspace.com/meditation/walking-meditation.

Walton, Alice G. (2015, February 9). "7 ways meditation can actually change the brain." Forbes. www.forbes.com/sites/alicegwalton/2015/02/09/7-ways-meditation-can-actually-change-the-brain/?sh=53c1df521465.

Weigardt, Liz. (n.d.). "5 steps for rewiring negative associations." Happy Brain Life. www.happybrainlife.com/blog/2019/2/21/5-steps-to-rewiring-negative-associations.

www.ingramcontent.com/pod-product-compliance
Lightning Source LLC
Chambersburg PA
CBHW021447070526
44577CB00002B/302